The Goodness of God in the Gift of Scripture

The Goodness of God in the Gift of Scripture

20 Meditations

Uche Anizor

CROSSWAY®
WHEATON, ILLINOIS

The Goodness of God in the Gift of Scripture: 20 Meditations

Published by Crossway
1300 Crescent Street
Wheaton, Illinois 60187

Cover design: David Fassett

Cover image: Getty Images, Rawpixel, and Wikimedia Commons

First printing 2026

Printed in the United States of America

Trade paperback ISBN: 979-8-8749-0428-9
ePub ISBN: 979-8-8749-0430-2
PDF ISBN: 979-8-8749-0429-6

Library of Congress Cataloging-in-Publication Data

Names: Anizor, Uche, 1976– author.
Title: The goodness of God in the gift of scripture : 20 meditations / Uche Anizor.
Description: Wheaton, Illinois : Crossway, 2026. | Includes bibliographical references and index.
Identifiers: LCCN 2025013412 (print) | LCCN 2025013413 (ebook) | ISBN 9798874904289 trade paperback | ISBN 9798874904296 pdf | ISBN 9798874904302 epub
Subjects: LCSH: Bible. Psalms, CXIX—Meditations | God (Christianity)—Goodness
Classification: LCC BS1430.54 .A55 2026 (print) | LCC BS1430.54 (ebook)
LC record available at https://lccn.loc.gov/2025013412
LC ebook record available at https://lccn.loc.gov/2025013413

Crossway is a publishing ministry of Good News Publishers.

BP 34 33 32 31 30 29 28 27 26
14 13 12 11 10 9 8 7 6 5 4 3 2 1

For Melissa,
true woman of the word

Contents

Introduction

Our Good God and the Grace of Scripture

THE TWENTIETH-CENTURY pastor and writer A. W. Tozer famously wrote, "What comes into our minds when we think about God is the most important thing about us. . . . Worship is pure or base as the worshiper entertains high or low thoughts of God." The shape of our worship and the course of our lives are dictated by our sense of what God is like. This conviction led Tozer to conclude that "the most portentous fact about any man is not what he at a given time may say or do, but what he in his deep heart conceives God to be like."[1]

I have often wondered if what Tozer said about our view of God is equally true regarding our view of Scripture, God's word. What comes into our minds when we think about the Bible?

Imagine you are playing one of those word games that requires you to give one-word clues to describe something. The word

1 A. W. Tozer, *The Knowledge of the Holy* (Lutterworth, 2022), 1.

Bible comes up on the next card. Assuming that you can't use a synonym like *Scripture,* what other words would you use to describe it? *Truth*? *Revelation*? *Rulebook*? *Law*? All valid descriptions. I wonder, however, if the word *gift* would be the first, second, or third thing that comes to mind for many of us. Certainly, most of us would affirm that Scripture is a gift—and we may highly esteem it—but *gift* would likely not be the first word association our minds would make. Yet making that association is incalculably important if we are going to approach God's word rightly.

I suspect that one of the main reasons we sometimes have difficulty putting God's word into practice or submitting to it joyfully is that we don't believe—in our heart of hearts—that it is good for us. If the Bible is somehow repressive or oppressive, why would we submit to its ways (especially if it actually *does* make life harder)? Behind our hesitancy regarding Scripture is often a cautious, though neither malicious nor brazen, distrust of God's goodness. But even when our trust in God appears relatively intact, we can still find ourselves resistant to Scripture's wisdom and demands. We fail to see it as a gift to embrace, as the grace of God itself and not merely a means of grace. We question if there is really a short- or long-term advantage to following God's sometimes-peculiar ways. And so we stop short of giving ourselves over fully to Scripture's teaching and, perhaps, pick and choose the elements of it that we, in our limited wisdom, see as making sense. In doing this, we cut ourselves off from the fullness of the grace that is Scripture—a grace that is manifold, rich, life-giving, and satisfying.

What comes into our minds when we think about God's word may prove to be the most important thing about us.

The Theme of Our Song

The simple affirmation of the goodness of God's word has been the refrain of God's people throughout the generations. The psalmist writes,

> Turn away the reproach that I dread,
> *for your rules are good.* (Ps. 119:39)

What underlies this affirmation is the basic belief that God is a kind ruler who gives good rules. As God and his word are inseparable (something we will come back to shortly), so the goodness of God and the goodness of Scripture are intertwined.

At the beginning of 2 Peter, we see the beautiful connection between the goodness of God and the gift of his word. Peter begins, "His divine power has given us everything required for life and godliness through the knowledge of him who called us by his own glory and goodness" (1:3 CSB). God, in the person of Jesus himself, has equipped us with everything we need to live godly lives, but access to these resources comes only through knowing him. He calls us into this knowledge out of his own glory and goodness. Peter continues, "By these he has given us very great and precious promises" (1:4a CSB). Animated by that same glory and goodness, Jesus gave us the promises of his word. In other words, the Scriptures are an overflow of God's goodness and gracious disposition toward us. The "great and precious promises" have a goal: "so that through them you may share in the divine nature, escaping the corruption that is in the world" (1:4b). God desires that we should reflect him—"share in the divine nature"—and this is for our ultimate and eternal good. To fulfill that goal, he gave us the Scriptures and its many promises. The goodness of God is expressed in the gift of Scripture.

John Calvin, after a careful exposition of how God reveals himself in creation, turns his attention to the Scriptures. He observes that while creation truly does furnish us with a knowledge of God, "it is needful that another and better help be added to direct us aright to the very Creator of the universe." God gave us the "privilege" of his word so that he might "become known unto salvation" and so that we might be gathered "more closely and intimately to himself." This, Calvin poetically concludes, "is a special gift, where God, to instruct the church, not merely uses mute teachers [i.e., the created order] but also opens his own most hallowed lips."[2] Creation is a gift, and God's self-disclosure in creation is a gift. But the greater grace is God opening his "hallowed lips" in Scripture to bring us into a clear-eyed knowledge of him. Scripture is the gift of clear sight to those who are largely blind.

Christians rightly acknowledge, extol, and even write hymns about the goodness of God in the gift of Scripture! The early twentieth century saw a number of such hymns written by evangelicals. For example, the second stanza of "Oh, Wonderful Word!" declares,

> Oh, wonderful, wonderful Word of the Lord!
> The lamp that our Father above

2 John Calvin, *Institutes of the Christian Religion*, ed. John T. McNeill, trans. Ford Lewis Battles, 2 vols., Library of Christian Classics 20–21 (Westminster John Knox, 2006), 1.6.1 (1:70).

So kindly has lighted to teach us the way
That leads to the arms of his love![3]

And another hymn, referring to Scripture, exclaims,

There Thy holy will we read,
There upon Thy grace we feed;
There find guidance for our way,
And correction when we stray.[4]

Notice the common themes of these songs. The wonderful word of the Lord was given out of God's kindness and mercy to lead us to his arms of love. By his good word, we feed on his grace. The word resounds with the loving heart of God. The giving of Scripture is the grace of God in concrete form. This, among other things, has always been a theme of our song as God's people.

God's Loving Verbal Presence

In lauding and praising the Scriptures, are we giving to a book the honor due to God alone? Are we committing bibliolatry, the supposed idolizing of the Bible? These questions have already been answered to some degree, but they are worth addressing more specifically. Perhaps the place to begin is Scripture, listening to the way it speaks of itself and following the connections it makes between God and his word.

In a song seeking God's protection from his enemies, the psalmist writes,

3 Fanny Crosby, "Oh, Wonderful Word!" (1887). Public domain.

4 H. F. Lyte, "Well Thy Works Proclaim Thee" (1911). Public domain.

In God, whose word I praise,
  in the LORD, whose word I praise,
in God I trust; I shall not be afraid. (Ps. 56:10–11)

On the surface, this is a very odd and unexpected coupling of items. "When I am afraid, I put my trust in God," says the psalmist. So far, so good. But rather than extolling the Lord who has delivered him, he repeats three times, "I praise God's word!" (56:4, 10 [2x]). Scripture clearly encourages, perhaps summons, us to praise God's word. The question becomes, "How do we do this in a way that always honors the Lord?"

When we affirm that Scripture is the word of God, we are saying that whenever Scripture speaks, God speaks. When Scripture speaks a word of comfort, God is speaking that word of comfort. When the Bible proclaims God's promises, we believe that God himself is proclaiming those words of promise. God is present wherever and whenever his word is read, spoken, prayed, or sung. But his presence is neither physical nor mystical; rather, his presence is verbal but no less real.

Imagine receiving a letter from a loved one who is thousands of miles away. While he is nowhere near you physically, every sentence of his letter makes him present to you. And his presence is neither merely imaginary nor in the form of memories that the letter evokes. Instead, because the letter is an expression of himself—his heart, his humor, his concerns—you are interacting with him as you read. The letter is an extension of him.

Or imagine waking up to a note on the kitchen table that reads, "Please take out the trash," written by your mother. At the risk of asking an obvious question, "Who is issuing the command?"

Certainly, it's not the note itself commanding you to do your chore. Rather, there is a person speaking to you, making her presence felt in the form of a scribbled-down note. To disregard her instruction would be to disregard her.

In a similar way, Scripture, as an articulate, clear, deliberate, and sufficient letter or note from God, is an extension of himself into our time and space and circumstance. Therefore, as one writer puts it, "To encounter the words of Scripture is to encounter God in action."[5] Or as Augustine counsels, "Treat the scripture of God as the face of God."[6] God and his word are inseparable. This is why it is entirely appropriate to sing love songs and hymns to God's word. God and his word together are our crown, our distinctive glory as his people. Do we believe this?

The Bible's Song About the Bible

My modest aim in this book is to help us retrieve a sense of the goodness of Scripture, to recapture the conviction that God's word to us is a gift given for our earthly and eternal happiness. My hope is that when we receive the Bible as grace to us, that attitude will foster a love and gratitude in our hearts for its encouragements and instructions.

This book comprises twenty brief meditations rooted mainly in Psalm 119, Scripture's own love song to Scripture. In each chapter's meditation, I do two things. First, I highlight one gift (or benefit) we receive from God's word. The psalmist sees Scripture

5 Timothy Ward, *Words of Life: Scripture as the Living and Active Word of God* (IVP Academic, 2009), 48.

6 Augustine, "Sermon 22.7," in *The Works of Saint Augustine*, part 3, *Homilies*, vol. 2, *Sermons 20–50 on the Old Testament*, trans. Edmund Hill (New City Press, 2009), 46.

as a gift that keeps on giving gifts—that is, a fountain of blessings from God. I have selected twenty such blessings, each chapter showcasing one. Second, I demonstrate that each benefit or act of blessing attributed to God's word in Psalm 119 is elsewhere, in the Bible, attributed to God himself. In highlighting this, I am trying to press home the wonderful truth that God, the source of all blessing, has chosen his word as the primary way to connect us to that blessing. His giving is often done through Scripture, and this should drive us to his word, eagerly expecting to receive good—not harm—from him.

I recommend reading each chapter meditatively rather than speeding through the book, perhaps reading one chapter each weekday over four weeks. Each chapter concludes with a song or prayer that you can either sing or say back to God. The goal here is love: to love God through loving his word, to so treasure God's speaking voice in Scripture that we would view it as more valuable than a new car or dream home. As the psalmist writes,

> The law of your mouth is better to me
> than thousands of gold and silver pieces. (Ps. 119:72)

> Therefore I love your commandments
> above gold, above fine gold. (119:127)

1

The Gift of Blessedness

Blessed are those whose way is blameless,
who walk in the law of the L*ORD*!
Blessed are those who keep his testimonies,
who seek him with their whole heart.

PSALM 119:1–2

THE FIRST WORD in the book of Psalms is "blessed." True blessedness is, in a sense, the theme of the Psalter. It is noteworthy, then, that the theme of blessedness in Psalm 1 is linked to our attitude toward God's law, and this is at the very beginning of Israel's songbook. This should grab our attention because it signals that the blessedness of being God's people—the blessedness *from* and *about* which we sing—is wonderfully connected to our relationship to his word.

Psalm 119—the longest psalm of all—begins similarly: "Blessed are those . . . / who walk in the law of the LORD! / . . . who keep his testimonies" (119:1–2). Blessedness is the theme of Psalm 119, and the psalm as a whole may be seen as an expanded meditation on the blessedness that comes through God's word. So it is fitting to pause and reflect on what it means to be "blessed."

#Blessed

I have a nagging sense that when we read the word *blessed*, we either feel indifferent or suspicious. Both of these responses are likely the result of the way the term is (over)used in our day-to-day lives. Scrolling through social media, you'll find pictures of people admiring themselves in the mirror with the caption "#Blessed." We see posts of luxurious spa days, beautiful vacations, acceptance letters to grad school, perfect family pictures—not to mention the extravagant exploits of countless celebrities—all tagged with "#Blessed." One writer remarks cynically,

> Calling something "blessed" has become the go-to term for those who want to boast about an accomplishment while pretending to be humble, fish for a compliment, acknowledge a success (without sounding too conceited), or purposely elicit envy. Blessed . . . is now used to explain that coveted Ted talk invite as well as to celebrate your grandmother's 91st birthday.[1]

In our culture, to be blessed is to have something you know many others would want or something you know is beyond the experience of the average person. This same writer quips,

1 Jessica Bennet, "They Feel 'Blessed,'" *New York Times*, May 2, 2014, https://www.nytimes.com/.

"There's nothing quite like invoking holiness as a way to brag about your life." While there are many examples of the term being used in appropriate and even humble ways, the omnipresence of its use, the things it is normally attached to, and the context in which it's used has largely cheapened what should be a rich and meaningful term. Does this way of understanding the blessed life have any connection to the biblical meaning of the word?

There are two Hebrew terms normally translated "blessed." The first, *baruk*, often refers to giving or receiving some kind of gift. In the creation account, the man and woman are "blessed" as those created in God's image and called to carry out his mandate (Gen. 1:28). Abraham is "blessed" as the partner in God's covenant (12:2). In this case, blessing is about bestowing gifts from one party to another. The second term, *ashre*, refers to the state of true happiness, and it is this term that we find here in Psalm 119, as well as in Psalm 1. Now being "blessed" (*baruk*) and being happy (*ashre*) are clearly related. The one who experiences true blessedness (*ashre*) is certainly someone blessed (*baruk*) by God. The terms overlap but are distinct. Outward blessing is not an automatic indicator that someone's life is truly blessed (*ashre*). Celebrity lives are a cautionary tale in this regard.

This is also the sense of blessedness we find in the Beatitudes. Our Lord says, "Blessed are those who mourn. . . . Blessed are those who are persecuted for righteousness' sake" (Matt. 5:4, 10). True happiness is not found in circumstances or in stuff. Mourning and persecution are not the kinds of things we would normally label with #Blessed. True happiness is being seen as we really are by God. In fact, true happiness *is* being connected to

God despite our situation or feelings. To be blessed is to experience fullness of life.

Sharing God's Triune Blessedness

In two astonishing passages, the apostle Paul describes God himself as *makarios*, which is the Greek term that translates the Hebrew *ashre* and means "blessed" or simply "happy." The apostle describes the good news as "the gospel of the glory of the *blessed* God" (1 Tim. 1:11) and God as "he who is the *blessed* and only Sovereign" (6:15). God is the happy God. He possesses perfect fullness of life in himself. This is his blessedness, and he wants to share this with us.

To be blessed is to experience fullness of life in communion with the triune God. C. S. Lewis writes, "The whole purpose for which we exist is to be thus taken into the life of God."[2] He adds, "The whole dance or drama or pattern of this three-Personal life is to be played out in each one of us: or (putting it the other way round) each one of us has got to enter that pattern, take his place in that dance. There is no other way to the happiness for which we were made."[3] We were made for blessedness, a happiness that has eternal and infinitely deep roots. Lewis depicts this happiness poetically as an intra-Trinitarian dance or drama, a shared love and delight that always exists among the three persons of the Godhead. It is unimaginably rich and all-satisfying, even if currently incomprehensible. God made us to be filled to overflowing with this kind of life. Ultimately, for the Christian, true blessedness is being "in Christ," which enables us to somehow experience this

2 C. S. Lewis, *Mere Christianity* (HarperOne, 2000), 161.
3 Lewis, *Mere Christianity*, 176.

intra-Trinitarian fullness of life. God desires to fill our lives out of the overflow of his blessedness. He made us and redeemed us to be really and truly happy.

We All Want to Be Happy

Everybody, rightly, wants to be happy. This legitimate human drive is not ignored or pooh-poohed by God. Instead, through the psalmist, he lays out for us the path to true happiness.

To begin, the psalmist writes, "Truly happy are those whose way is blameless—namely, those who walk in the law of Yahweh!" (Ps. 119:1 AT). This verse parallels Psalm 1 in repeating the refrain of blessedness coming to those who walk in the way of torah. The word *law* here is taken by many to mean "instruction" and it includes all of God's revelation. Happy are those who obey the Lord's instruction and follow his guidance and teaching. An autonomous, self-reliant life does not lead to happiness. It is noteworthy that blamelessness is paralleled with obedience to God's instruction. The psalmist makes a similar move in the second verse: "Truly happy are those who keep his testimonies—that is, those who seek him with their whole heart" (119:2 AT). There is no mystery to what it means to seek the Lord wholeheartedly. It is to "keep" his testimonies, which means to observe or put into practice the decrees of God.

Yet Scripture is abundantly clear that blessedness comes from God. *He* is the bestower of true happiness. Here are several examples:

> Blessed is the one whose transgression is forgiven,
> whose sin is covered. (Ps. 32:1)

> Blessed is the nation whose God is the Lord,
> the people whom he has chosen as his heritage! (33:12)

> Blessed is the man who takes refuge in him! (34:8)

> Blessed is the one you choose and bring near. (65:4)

> Blessed are those whose strength is in you. (84:5)

> Blessed are the people to whom such blessings fall!
> Blessed are the people whose God is the Lord! (144:15)

> Blessed are you when others revile you and persecute you and utter all kinds of evil against you falsely on my account. Rejoice and be glad, for your reward is great in heaven. (Matt. 5:11–12)

Blessed (Heb. *ashre*, Gk. *makarios*) are those who are forgiven, protected, brought near, chosen, strengthened, and rewarded *by God*! These benefits and privileges are just a few dimensions of the blessed life. These passages could be multiplied tenfold. And it is not headline news that God is the source of this blessedness. Psalm 119 is a poetic and devotional exploration of the many dimensions of the blessed life given graciously by God. But we are to keep in mind that God, the giver of blessedness, often does not work alone, so to speak. He uses a gift to give his other gifts. "Blessed are those . . . *who walk in the law of the Lord*" (Ps. 119:1). The life of true happiness that we crave, the life of fullness that God desires to give, is bestowed to us through the means of his good word. Those who give earnest attention to his law and devote their whole hearts to knowing and following it can expect true blessedness, both now and forevermore.

How happy they who know the Lord,
With whom he deigns to dwell!
He feeds and cheers them by his word,
His arm supports them well.

Wandering in sin, our souls he found,
And bid us seek his face;
Gave us to hear the gospel sound,
And taste the gospel grace.

His presence sweetens all their cares,
And makes their burdens light;
A word from him dispels their fears,
And breaks the gloom of night.

Let us enjoy and highly prize
These tokens of thy love:
Till thou shalt bid our spirits rise,
To worship thee above.

JOHN NEWTON
"O Happy They Who Know the Lord"
1779

2
The Gift of Purity

How can a young man keep his way pure?
By guarding it according to your word. . . .
I have stored up your word in my heart,
that I might not sin against you.

PSALM 119:9, 11

PURITY HAS FALLEN ON HARD TIMES.

Exhibit A: In recent years, there's been a bit of a backlash against "purity culture"—namely, the supposed overemphasis on sexual purity, abstinence, courtship, and the like, which pervaded evangelical churches in the 1990s. Despisers of so-called purity culture claim that these emphases are, at best, only partially biblical and, in most cases, seriously harmful to those who adopt its tenets. One writer, reflecting on her past experience of purity culture, laments, "I felt embarrassed realizing that so much of what I had accepted as true had nothing to do with biblical sexuality or the grace of

God."[1] Purity culture is, thus, in need of a reckoning. Yet in the aftermath of this full onslaught against purity culture, we are in danger (and are sometimes guilty) of making purity itself a byword. If calling young people to a life of purity produces a visceral response—a cringe—then we've likely already crossed that line.

Exhibit B: Legalism is often seen as the most important danger preventing Christians from making progress or experiencing joy in their Christian faith. Pastor Kevin DeYoung describes our situation:

> Among conservative Christians there is sometimes the mistaken notion that if we are truly gospel-centered we won't talk about rules or imperatives or moral exertion. We are so eager not to confuse indicatives (what God has done) and imperatives (what we should do) that we get leery of letting biblical commands lead uncomfortably to conviction of sin. We're scared of words like diligence, effort, and duty. Pastors don't know how to preach the good news in their sermons and still strongly exhort churchgoers to cleanse themselves from every defilement of body and spirit (2 Cor. 7:1). We know legalism (salvation by law keeping) and antinomianism (salvation without the need for law keeping) are both wrong, but antinomianism feels like a much safer danger.[2]

Think of the number of times you have heard or read something like, "You can't earn favor with God!" or "God is not calling us to pull up our bootstraps" (whatever these are) or "You need to

1 Rachel Joy Welcher, "What Comes After the Purity Culture Reckoning," *Christianity Today*, October 14, 2021, https://www.christianitytoday.com/.

2 Kevin DeYoung, *The Hole in Our Holiness: Filling the Gap Between Gospel Passion and the Pursuit of Godliness* (Crossway, 2012), 19.

stop striving," and so forth. These are all well-intentioned messages. But an unintended consequence is that they foster the notion that God is not primarily concerned about our holiness or purity. Instead, he's mainly concerned that we know we are loved and accepted.

Purity is getting a bad rap these days.

The Shared Human Drive

Yet as much as we try to downplay or question the importance of purity, there is no evading the primitive human sense that we have a need for it. Religions as far apart as we can imagine share a common belief that, in some way, we must be cleansed. During the Pitcher Festival (or Kumbh Mela), tens of millions of Hindus bathe in the filthy waters of the Ganges. They believe that if they bathe, especially on certain days, they will be cleansed of sins—and even end the cycle of reincarnation. This kind of practice is repeated daily by millions. At certain locations along the Ganges, the waters are so laden with bacteria that government officials strongly warn against bathing there. Yet the desperation for cleansing is so strong that people risk grave sickness in order to be purified.

Purity is also woven into the fabric of the Jewish faith. You cannot read the Old Testament without noticing what seems like an obsession with distinctions between clean and unclean, pure and impure, holy and common. The Israelites were considered holy, simply by virtue of being in covenant with God. This holiness was initiated and maintained by God's taking them to himself as his treasured possession. God is the sanctifier. Yet they were also called to "be holy, for I the Lord your God am holy" (Lev. 19:2).

By following God's moral and ritual instructions, they would show themselves as holy, thus reflecting the character of their God.

Clean/unclean or pure/impure primarily defined the ritual standing of people. Those who were pure had access to God in the tabernacle. Those who were impure, through disobedience or contact with an impure thing, had to be ritually cleansed in order to gain (or regain) that access. As long as people, after becoming defiled, availed themselves of God's means of cleansing, they would remain faithful members of God's holy people. While guarding the sanctuary from defilement, the laws of ritual purity were daily reminders of what was required to approach their holy God. For the Israelites, their highest good was bound up with their purity.

This sentiment is repeated in an arresting statement from the author of Hebrews, lest we think purity and holiness are solely Old Testament things: "Strive for peace with everyone, *and for the holiness without which no one will see the Lord*" (Heb. 12:14). There are no two ways about it: holiness is, in some sense, essential to salvation. J. C. Ryle, commenting on this passage, affirms, "If unsanctified souls can be saved and go to heaven, the Bible is not true."[3] He later adds, "Alas, what searching, sifting words are these! . . . Surely it is a text that ought to make us consider our ways, and search our hearts. Surely it should raise within us solemn thoughts, and send us to prayer."[4] "Strive for holiness!" the author of Hebrews implores. Paul exhorts Timothy to set an example of purity (1 Tim. 4:12) and young women "to be

3 J. C. Ryle, *Holiness: Its Nature, Hindrances, Difficulties, and Roots* (Charles Nolan, 2001), 38–39.

4 Ryle, *Holiness*, 55.

self-controlled, pure" (Titus 2:5). Paul's ministry is centered on presenting the church as a "pure virgin to Christ" (2 Cor. 11:2). James is concerned about "pure and undefiled" religion (James 1:27), while Peter calls the church to "respectful and pure conduct" before nonbelievers (1 Pet. 3:2). John talks about how our ultimate, eschatological purity—mirroring Christ's own purity—is the motivation for a life pursuing purity (1 John 3:3). And believers in heavenly glory are regularly portrayed in Revelation as clothed in pure garments (Rev. 15:6; 19:8, 14). It's clear that purity is not an incidental feature of the Christian vision of life.

So whether Hindu, Israelite, Christian, or otherwise, God's revelation in our consciences and in his word bears witness to the fact that we need to be cleansed. We know that purity, in some way, is the path to life.

Keeping Our Way Pure

In light of this very common human need to be cleansed and in the face of God's covenant law, the psalmist in our passage poses one of the most important questions one can ask: "How can a young man keep his way pure?" (Ps. 119:9a). In other words, the psalmist is asking, "How do I live a life that keeps me close to God, enjoying the nearness of fellowship available to those who have access to the tabernacle? How do I live a life reflective of the holiness granted to me through my covenantal bond to the Lord? How do I ongoingly mirror God's holiness in my day-to-day life?" This passage is beautiful in its simplicity, both of the question and the answer. Young men are typically understood in Scripture as being susceptible to certain youthful lusts and prone to folly. How does one at such a tender, precarious, and formative stage pursue the pure path? The answer—he must "cleanse his way," as the King James Version puts it, by "guarding it according to" God's word (119:9b ESV). Other translations focus on staying on the *path* by living according to God's word (NIV), while others stress holding fast to or heeding the word itself (CSB). Both senses are true and are captured well by Charles Spurgeon in his classic work on the Psalms:

> Young man, the Bible must be your chart, and you must exercise great watchfulness that your way may be according to its directions. You must take heed to your daily life as well as study your Bible, and you must study your Bible that you may take heed to your daily life. With the greatest care a man will go astray if his map misleads him; but with the most accurate map he will still lose his road if he does not take heed to it. The narrow way was never hit upon by chance, neither did any heedless man ever lead a holy life. We can sin without thought, we have only to neglect the great salvation and ruin our souls; but to obey the Lord and walk uprightly will need all our heart and soul and mind. Let the careless remember this.[5]

The presence of God's word, coupled with vigilance in knowing and heeding it, will keep both young and old pure in their way. Left on our own, we will drift toward sin and folly.

This is why the psalmist goes on to say, "I have stored up your word in my heart, / that I might not sin against you" (119:11).

5 Charles H. Spurgeon, *The Treasury of David*, 7 vols. (Zondervan, 1968), 3:157.

The word of God is like a treasure locked up in a safe, like a pearl of great price worthy of selling everything to own. The word, when treasured, is a defense against sin—especially as it is used by God to shape our affections and actions. John Calvin writes,

> If we do not imbibe the doctrine of God, and are well acquainted with it, Satan will easily surprise and entangle us in his meshes. Our true safeguard, then, lies not in a slender knowledge of his law, or in a careless perusal of it, but in hiding it deeply in our hearts. Here we are reminded, that however men may be convinced of their own wisdom, they are yet destitute of all right judgment, except as far as they have God as their teacher.[6]

In his characteristically punchy way, Spurgeon summarizes the psalmist's spiritual instruction: "His heart would be kept by the word because he kept the word in his heart."[7] How? By meditating on it—that is, singing it, thinking about it, reciting it, memorizing it, listening to it, reading and rereading it (see Ps. 1:2). By looking at it from every angle as if it were as precious to us as the ring was to Gollum in Tolkien's volumes.

Back to the Giver

The psalmist's theology of word-centered sanctification is repeated in the New Testament. The apostle Peter writes in his letter, "Having purified your souls by your obedience to the

6 John Calvin, *Psalms 93–150*, in *Commentary on the Book of Psalms*, trans. James Anderson, in *Calvin's Commentaries* (Baker, 2003), 4:409.

7 Spurgeon, *Treasury of David*, 3:159.

truth" (1 Pet. 1:22). The believers have purified their souls by means of obedience to God's word. In fact, Peter goes on to say that they were "born again," made new through the word of God (1:23). The word of God, when we are obedient to it, purifies us.

Yet the apostle Paul, in his blessing of the Thessalonian believers, writes, "Now may the God of peace himself sanctify you completely, and may your whole spirit and soul and body be kept blameless at the coming of our Lord Jesus Christ" (1 Thess. 5:23). He, like the Old Testament writers, views our sanctification as chiefly God's work. God makes us new. God alone cleanses us. By placing these two biblical emphases together—our self-cleansing and God's cleansing of us—it should be clear that we are encountering a familiar pattern, one that is repeated throughout this book: God works through his appointed means.

Imagine you are washing your car. You take out the hose, turn on the water, and start firing away at weeks of caked-on mud and bug splatter. Who is washing the car? You are. What is washing the car? The water. The water does not wash the car without you, nor is the car cleansed without the water. Both are, in fact, washing the car: one as the agent, the other as the means—but they are inseparable. So it is with Scripture. God is the purifier. The psalmist bears witness to this elsewhere (cf. Ps. 119:10). Yet God purifies us through our engagement with Scripture. In other words, the gift of purity comes to us through the gift of Scripture.

—

How shall the young direct their way?
What light shall be their perfect guide?
Thy word, O LORD, will safely lead,
if in its wisdom they confide.

Sincerely I have sought thee, Lord,
O let me not from Thee depart;
to know Thy will and keep from sin
Thy word I cherish in my heart.

AUTHOR UNKNOWN
"How Shall the Young Direct Their Way?"
1912

3

The Gift of No Shame

Oh that my ways may be steadfast
in keeping your statutes!
Then I shall not be put to shame,
having my eyes fixed on all your
commandments. . . .

I cling to your testimonies, O Lord;
let me not be put to shame!
PSALM 119:5–6, 31

IS SHAME A GOOD THING or a bad thing? What do you think? On the one hand, we are often told that we should never shame another person. There are few crimes worse than shaming someone because of some characteristic, especially one over which that person may have had no control. This is what one author calls our "anti-shame zeitgeist."[1] On the other hand, we live in

1 Joseph Burgo, "Challenging the Anti-Shame Zeitgeist," *The Atlantic*, June 17, 2013, https://www.theatlantic.com/.

a self-righteous shaming culture, where the virtuous thing is to shame whoever does not stand up for the cause of the day or whoever represents some group that "everyone" recognizes as evil. Our culture is confused. Shaming is seen as both wrong and right, cruel and virtuous.

Christians are sometimes even more confused about shame. In some circles, the idea of having a positive view of shame is completely out of the question. Shame is something Christ has borne for us (whatever that might mean to us); therefore, we should never feel shame or make someone else feel shame. I often ask my students, "Should Christians feel guilt for doing something wrong?" The unanimous answer in the classroom is yes. But when I ask, "Should Christians feel shame for wrongdoing?" only a few hands go up and many heads go down, followed by a few muffled and timid attempts to give the answer they think their professor wants to hear. Shame can be a confusing category. What are we to make of it? How are we to be oriented toward it?

Naming Shame

Shame is often seen primarily as a psychological concept. One New Testament scholar defines it as "the painful emotion that arises from an awareness that one has fallen short of some standard, ideal, or goal."[2] Shame is a negative feeling that comes from missing some valued standard, whether from God, family, or society.

Ed Welch, a noted psychologist, offers these two helpful definitions: "Shame is the deep sense that you are unaccept-

2 Te-Li Lau, *Defending Shame: Its Formative Power in Paul's Letters* (Baker Academic, 2020), 29.

able because of something you did, something done to you, or something associated with you. You feel exposed and humiliated." Then he strengthens and clarifies this further, noting that with shame "you are disgraced because you acted less than human, you were treated as if you were less than human, or you were associated with something less than human, and there are witnesses."[3] In these definitions, Welch draws attention to another central aspect of shame: the presence of witnesses. While shame is undoubtedly an internal experience—a feeling—it is equally, perhaps even primarily, a social experience. Philosopher Gregg Ten Elshof writes,

> The experience of shame always involves the sense of diminished social standing—the experience of losing significance in the company of respected others. . . . We experience ourselves as a source of pain, discomfort, inconvenience, or embarrassment for ourselves and for others. For this reason, shame usually causes the desire to shrink, to hide, or to disappear altogether.[4]

Shame is public embarrassment, humiliation, discomfort, disgrace. There is loss of social standing, real and/or perceived.

These definitions help us grasp, in broad strokes, aspects of the Bible's portrayal of shame. Scripture's picture of shame is multilayered, and wrapping our minds around it will help us better grasp the heart of the psalmist's prayer.

3 Edward T. Welch, *Shame Interrupted: How God Lifts the Pain of Worthlessness and Rejection* (New Growth Press, 2012), 2.

4 Gregg Ten Elshof, *For Shame: Rediscovering the Virtues of a Maligned Emotion* (Zondervan Reflective, 2021), 3.

A Kaleidoscope

Shame is a prevalent theme in the Bible. You find variations of the word used well over two hundred times throughout the Old and New Testaments. And its use is so rich and diverse that there are more than a dozen ways in which the experience is described. All these descriptions of shame are undoubtedly related, but seeing the vast array and the subtle nuances are helpful in filling out our picture of shame and showing us with greater clarity how God interacts with it. So at the risk of being overly thorough, shame is

- a feeling of embarrassment that should accompany sin (Isa. 1:29; 20:5; Jer. 3:3; 6:15, 8:12);
- a feeling of embarrassment that should accompany acting in ways that may not be sinful but distasteful or not befitting our calling (2 Sam. 6:20);
- not wanting to be associated with someone or others not wanting to associate with us (Mark 8:38; Luke 9:26; 1 Pet. 4:16);
- a final judgment of separation and dissociation from God (Mark 8:38; Luke 9:26);
- disgrace before others of our own group (2 Chron. 32:21; Isa. 66:5; Jer. 3:25);
- being disgraced before our enemies or outsiders (Neh. 1:3; Ps. 25:1–3, 19–20);
- being consumed by enemies and not being delivered by God (Pss. 31:1, 15–17; 44:9–16);
- being thwarted and opposed by God as an enemy (Pss. 35:4, 26; 40:13–15; 53:5; 57:3; 70:2–3; 71:24);

- the result of God opposing his people because of disobedience (Ps. 78:65–66);
- to appear lacking in terms of God's favor and provision (Pss. 37:18–19; 127:5);
- bringing embarrassment to others who are associated with us (Ps. 69:6; Prov. 10:5; 12:4; 28:7; 29:15);
- being mocked because of faithfulness to God (Ps. 69:6–10);
- being reproached and abandoned by others (Ps. 69:19–20);
- being seen as worthless and despicable by others (Ps. 71:13);
- when the tables are turned, God making his enemies look foolish for misconstruing his lack of favor on his people (Pss. 6:10; 86:17);
- being stripped of glory and splendor (Ps. 89:44–45);
- being scorned because of our weakness (Ps. 109:24–29);
- making oneself look foolish or stupid (Prov. 18:13); and
- public disgrace because of our circumstances or hardships (Isa. 54:4).

This list is by no means comprehensive (although you may think it is *too* comprehensive!). Also, while this list does not provide a strict definition of shame, it offers something far better. It provides a kaleidoscopic, or many-angled, view of what shame is about biblically. Through these descriptions, we get a fuller sense of the feelings and situations associated with it. There are three possible "audiences" involved in shame: God, God's people, and those outside. When we are put to shame, we are exposed and disgraced before God (because of sin). Publicly, we are put to shame for different reasons, depending on which public is in view. We are shamed before God's people for failing to meet biblical standards. But before those outside the church, we are shamed for failing to meet nonbiblical, and often antibiblical, standards. The former happens because of sin; the latter, often, because of obedience.

Don't Let Me Be Shamed!

Now with our minds filled with shame—the biblical categories, that is—we return to Psalm 119.

In our psalm, the social situation of the writer is unclear. There seems to be some form of hardship or oppression but of what kind is uncertain. We can, however, imagine—and indeed get hints of—a number of the scenarios described in our list being of concern to the psalmist. He may want to avoid the shame that accompanies sin, or being mocked for his faithfulness, or being disgraced before his enemies, or lacking God's favor. Nevertheless, in the face of his circumstances, he prays, "Help me be faithful and steady in keeping your statutes, then I won't be put to shame, for I am fully committed to your commandments" (Ps. 119:5–6 AT). If the psalmist remains fixed on following God's word, he can be confident that he will be ultimately vindicated, honored, and not disgraced. Passive neglect of God's word, as well as active disobedience to it, can lead to shame before God (in the first case) and sometimes even before other people (in the second case). The psalmist, as one commentator puts it, "must contemplate with favor all that God has commanded, not selecting what he prefers but obeying completely what the Lord has required."[5]

5 Daniel J. Estes, *Psalms 73–150*, The New American Commentary (B&H, 2019), 403.

The second passage is similar. He simply cries out, "Lord, I cling to your testimonies, don't let me be disgraced" (119:31 AT). One can imagine a situation where the psalmist's oppressors—whether individual or national—mock him for his wholehearted and clingy commitment to God's word. These enemies may scoff at the value of trusting God and his word. Walking with God may appear to be counterproductive, especially in the face of the psalmist's hardships. But it is on the basis of his being glued to God's law that he makes his appeal with confidence that God would prevent him from looking foolish. Confidence in the face of shame comes from clinging to God's word.

These prayers of the psalmist make clear the biblical theme that God is the lifter of our shame. There is no one else to appeal to in the face of shame. The prophet Isaiah records a beautiful promise:

> Do not be afraid; you will not be put to shame.
> Do not fear disgrace; you will not be humiliated.
> You will forget the shame of your youth
> and remember no more the reproach of your widowhood.
> For your Maker is your husband—
> the Lord Almighty is his name—
> the Holy One of Israel is your Redeemer;
> he is called the God of all the earth. (Isa. 54:4–5 NIV)

Elsewhere, God makes his shame-lifter role clear when he promises to Israel,

> And my people shall never again be put to shame.
> You shall know that I am in the midst of Israel,

> and that I am the LORD your God and there is none else.
> And my people shall never again be put to shame.
> (Joel 2:26–27)

The Lord in our midst is the guarantee that we will not carry shame forever. "No one who hopes in you," says the psalmist, "will *ever* be put to shame" (Ps. 25:3 NIV). And the apostle Paul, reflecting on Isaiah 28:16 and speaking of Christ, writes, "Everyone who believes in him will not be put to shame" (Rom. 10:11).

God rescues us from shame by restoring lost things, reversing tragedy, redeeming lost years, and even removing those things that bring public disgrace. He promises those who trust in him freedom from many facets of the shame outlined above: his embarrassment of us, others triumphing over us, lost glory, ultimate weakness, looking foolish, or facing God's opposition. Instead of shame, he offers justification, vindication, and full salvation. In doing this, he not only takes care of our external circumstances but also addresses the feelings associated with shame, like fear and humiliation—again, for all those who hope and trust in him.

Shame and the Word

This emphasis on trusting the Lord brings us back to our psalm and the emphasis of this book. When the apostle Paul says that all who trust in Christ will not be put to shame, he immediately ties this to the preaching and hearing of the gospel: "Faith comes from hearing the word preached about Christ" (Rom. 10:17 AT). It is clear that to trust in Christ (the one who experienced our public shame) or to hope in God is to hold to his promises and cling to his word. Thus when Scripture says that no one who trusts in him will be put to shame, it effectively means that anyone who stays steadfast in his word can have confidence that they will not be disgraced or distanced from God's favor.

As God's people, we are always in danger of looking foolish in the midst of whichever cultural context we find ourselves. Shame is always knocking at our door. We are always on the cusp of public disgrace. Yet we access the ongoing freedom from both the reality and feelings of shame through adhering to his word—words that promise no shame to his own, words that keep us faithful to our covenant Lord.

—

I'm not ashamed to own my Lord,
or to defend his cause,
maintain the honor of his Word,
the glory of his cross.

Jesus, my God! I know his name,
his name is all my trust;
nor will he put my soul to shame,
nor let my hope be lost.

ISAAC WATTS
"At the Cross!"
1911

4

The Gift of a Wonderful Counselor

Your testimonies are my delight;
they are my counselors.

PSALM 119:24

THE VERY FIRST PSALM begins with a warning about the counsel we keep. The psalmist writes,

> Blessed is the man
> who walks not in the counsel of the wicked. (Ps. 1:1)

The truly happy man is careful about whom he takes to be his counselors. Rather than denying our need for counselors altogether, the psalmist reminds us that the counsel we keep has the power to set our lives either on a fruitful trajectory or on a path to destruction.

The story of Rehoboam, king Solomon's son, illustrates this well. After Solomon died, the people of Israel were set on crowning Rehoboam as king. A party of leaders approach the soon-to-be-ruler, asking him to lighten the heavy burdens Solomon had placed on the people. Rehoboam receives their request but asks for time to consider it carefully. During that time, he consults with the older men who had counseled his father. They tell him to lighten the people's burdens because, in doing so, he would win over their hearts. Instead, he abandons the counsel of the elder advisors and turns to the counsel of a group of young men he grew up with. Rather than encouraging him to respond kindly, they prod him to put the people in their place.

So after three days of mulling the matter over and seeking counsel, Rehoboam responds to the people, "My father made your yoke heavy, but I will add to your yoke; my father disciplined you with whips, but I will discipline you with barbed whips" (1 Kings 12:14 CSB). When the people saw that they made no impression on Rehoboam, they gave up on the whole house of David and no longer submitted to that line of kings. The author of Kings summarizes, "So Israel has been in rebellion against the house of David to this day" (12:19).

Two sets of counselors, two destinies. Rehoboam's poor choice of counselors affected the course of many lives—kingdoms even—not just his own. So it is with us. Who will be our counselors?

Scripture often reiterates that good counsel is a good thing. We read in the book of Proverbs,

> Where there is no guidance, a people falls,
> but in an abundance of counselors there is safety.
> (Prov. 11:14)

Without counsel plans fail,
but with many advisers they succeed. (15:22)

Plans are established by counsel;
by wise guidance wage war. (20:18)

For by wise guidance you can wage your war,
and in abundance of counselors there is victory. (24:6)

Our need for counsel is an admission that we are not omniscient; it is an acknowledgement that we are not God. The apostle Paul asks rhetorically,

For who has known the mind of the Lord,
or who has been his counselor? (Rom. 11:34)

The implied answer is "Nobody." God is the only one who has no need for counselors.

To be human, then, is to be counsel-dependent. Sometimes we lack perspective; sometimes we simply lack information; sometimes we lack experience; sometimes we have tunnel vision or blind spots. Whatever the reason, we are creatures who need counsel. We were never meant to go it alone. We need peers and sages, people who know us well, and those who do not but can give us an outside perspective. We need an abundance and an array of counselors.

Wonder of a Counselor

A description of the Messiah that we may not regularly emphasize comes from the famous Christmas passage in Isaiah 9:6: "And his name shall be called Wonderful Counselor." We tend to focus on the other marvelous descriptions of Christ ("Mighty God," "Prince of Peace") that we may miss this very meaningful dimension of Christ's messianic ministry to us. "Wonderful Counselor" is translated literally as "wonder of a counselor," pointing to the truth that he possesses something far beyond human wisdom.[1] Isaiah applies to Christ a description that is reminiscent of an attribute he elsewhere ascribes to God:

> This also comes from the LORD of hosts;
> he is wonderful in counsel
> and excellent in wisdom. (Isa. 28:29)

In Christ are "hidden all the treasures of wisdom and knowledge" (Col. 2:3). According to the ancient writer John Chrysostom, the Messiah is a wonder of a counselor "because of his many other teachings, but especially because he revealed his Father to humankind."[2] Calvin says of the Lord, "He is in every respect the highest and most perfect teacher" since "all that is necessary for salvation is opened up by Christ."[3] In other words, all that we must know for our temporal and eternal happiness is hidden in Christ.

In a sermon entitled, "His Name—The Counsellor," the young Charles Spurgeon describes three ways Christ is to be seen as the counselor—and this is much in line with the long history of

1 John N. Oswalt, *The Book of Isaiah, Chapters 1–39* (Eerdmans, 1986), 247.

2 John Chrysostom, *Homilies on the Gospel of John 81*, in *Isaiah 1–39*, Ancient Christian Commentary on Scripture, Old Testament, vol. 10, ed. Steven A. McKinion (IVP Academic, 2014), 74.

3 John Calvin, *Commentary on the Book of the Prophet Isaiah*, trans. William Pringle, in *Calvin's Commentaries* (Baker, 2003), 1:310.

Christian thought on Isaiah 9:6.[4] First, being God himself, he stands in the eternal counsel with God; he is a counselor with God. Second, he is the messenger of the counsel, the one who makes the will of the eternal divine counsel known to us. Third, "Christ is a Counsellor to us and with us, because we can consult with him, and he doth counsel and advise us as to the right way and the path of peace." It is this third dimension of Christ's counseling role that is most important for our reflection.

Spurgeon expands on what it means for Christ to be a counselor to us by highlighting three features of his role. First, Christ is a *necessary* counselor. He is the one whom we must consult in all things if we are to find success in life: "So sure as we do anything without asking counsel of God we fall into trouble." There is no other counselor that we can describe as absolutely necessary except Christ. Second, Christ is a *faithful* counselor. Unlike some counselors, he does not counsel out of self-interest but will always guide us toward what is best for us. Third, Christ is a *hearty* counselor. He is not a detached advisor but one who cares deeply about us. To help us grasp what Christ's counsel is like, Spurgeon contrasts it with that of a lawyer. He writes of the latter,

> He [the lawyer] is as cool as possible; you think you are asking counsel of a block of marble. No doubt his advice will come out all right at last, and it is pretty certain it will be good for you; but it is not hearty. He does not enter into the sympathies of the matter with you. What is it to him whether you succeed

4 The following is drawn from Charles H. Spurgeon, "His Name—The Counsellor," September 26, 1858, in *New Park Street Pulpit*, vol. 4, https://www.spurgeon.org/.

> or not—whether the object of your heart shall be accomplished or not. It is but a professional interest he takes.

But of Christ, he exclaims, "Oh! for a Counsellor that could tie your heart into unison with his own! Now Christ is such a Counsellor as that. He is a hearty Counsellor. His interests and your interests are bound up together, and he is hearty with you."

We all want sound counsel; but we would prefer sound counsel coupled with loving empathy. We want someone to care, even as they try to give the best advice they can. This is what we receive and more from the Wonderful Counselor. The necessary, faithful, and hearty counsel of Christ is none other than the counsel of God himself. And we encounter this counsel most readily when we sit at the feet of Scripture.

The Men of My Counsel

The thing I enjoy most about my job as a theology professor is the opportunity to counsel students in everything from theology to family issues to dating relationships to career guidance. It is a privilege that students entrust themselves to me, believing they will receive sound advice. Yet while I try my best to listen to them, to understand their situation and concerns, and to speak biblically, I have no delusions that my counsel is always the best. My knowledge of the situation is partial. My knowledge of Scripture is not exhaustive. My range of experiences is limited. My perspective may be skewed by my own interests or background. In short, I am not the deepest well from which to draw.

The psalmist writes of God's law,

> *Your* testimonies are my delight;
> *they* are my counselors. (Ps. 119:24)

One translator renders the verse, "Yes, your precepts are my delight, my constant counselors." He further notes that "my constant counselors" can be translated literally as "the men of my counsel."[5] God's precepts are personified as a group of men from whom the psalmist eagerly and regularly takes counsel. He doesn't trust in his own judgment or lean solely on his own understanding but comes to the word for direction and redirection.

Counsel has everything to do with how we live a God-pleasing and prudent life regardless of the circumstances. Just as there is both good and bad counsel from people, there is good and bad counsel from within. We *can* take counsel within ourselves (Ps. 13:2), but since we are sometimes self-deceived, we must be wary of that counsel, especially if it has to do with something our hearts so desperately desire. Instead, we can have confidence in God's word as our counselor, trusting that it will never lead us astray. The deepest well that we must always come back to and draw from is Scripture itself. We must make Scripture our constant counselor. In fact, it is only when Scripture is our constant counselor that we can discern the wisdom and folly of our human counselors.

The Revealed Heart of the Counselor

God's word is our counselor. Jesus is our counselor. God is our counselor. All these are true statements, but how do they fit together? I think it is best to see Scripture as an expression of the kind heart of

5 Robert Alter, *The Book of Psalms* (W. W. Norton and Company, 2007), 422.

the Wonderful Counselor. This counselor does not guide primarily through whispers in our hearts or ineffable moments of ecstasy (though he certainly could). This counselor counsels through the counsel of his word. If we want to experience this underemphasized aspect of Christ's ministry, we must, as C. S. Lewis once noted, steep ourselves in the "tone or temper" of Scripture.[6] We must become at home with its twists and turns, its likes and dislikes. In the end, we must take his word as the "men of our counsel," as our constant companion.

Where'er I go, whate'er my task,
The counsel of my God I ask,
Who ruleth all things right;
Unless He give both thought and deed,
The utmost pains can ne'er succeed,
And vain must be man's might.

I lean upon His mighty arm,
Which shieldeth me from every harm
And all calamity;
If in His precepts I shall live,
Whate'er is useful He will give;
Nothing can injure me.

PAUL FLEMMING
"Where'er I Go, Whate'er My Task"
1881

6 C. S. Lewis, *Reflections on the Psalms* (Fount, 1978), 94.

5

The Gift of Fear

Confirm to your servant your promise,
that you may be feared. . . .

I am a companion of all who fear you,
of those who keep your precepts.

PSALM 119:38, 63

IT MIGHT SEEM like a strange thing, in a book about God's gifts, to include fear as one of those graces. When we think about fear, we tend to view it as something we'd rather not have any acquaintance with, unless we're talking about that strange delight that some take in getting scared by a horror movie or gravity-defying roller coaster. We try generally to avoid things that provoke fear. A pounding heart and cold sweat seem like anything but a gift.

The Christian mind, one attentive to Scripture, is trained to think about fear in two ways. On the one hand, we are told, "There is no fear in love, but perfect love casts out fear. For fear has to do with punishment, and whoever fears has not been perfected in love" (1 John 4:18). Fear in the context of faith in the God of the gospel is a flaw, something to be overcome. On the other hand, we are also told things like,

> The fear of the LORD is the beginning of knowledge,
> fools despise wisdom and instruction. (Prov. 1:7)

Fear is virtuous and something to be cultivated. Michael Reeves, in his helpful book on the fear of God, comments that these two ways of approaching fear sometimes coalesce into two different camps within the Christian universe: one focuses on God's love and emphasizes the unhelpfulness of fear; the other delights in God's grandeur and his worthiness, which are to be feared.[1] In the first case, fear is clearly not a gift. We may, however, with much persuasion, get our minds to concede that fear in the face of God's awesomeness is a *kind of* gift, just not a very exciting one.

Enter Jesus to clear the confusion. The prophet Isaiah writes of the Messiah to come,

> And the Spirit of the LORD shall rest upon him, . . .
> And his delight shall be in the fear of the LORD.
> (Isa. 11:2, 3)

If any doubt lingers in our minds about the goodness of fear, look to Jesus (and the Spirit). The Spirit of God rests on Jesus, and we

1 Michael Reeves, *Rejoice and Tremble: The Surprising Good News of the Fear of the Lord* (Crossway, 2021), 13–17.

assume that this same Spirit produces in the Messiah a delight in the fear of the Lord. Healthy people do not usually delight in things that are harmful to them. Holy people do not usually delight in things that are wrong. We delight in gifts—things that are good, beneficial, and, well, delightful! Here we have the Messiah delighting in the fear of the Lord. Therefore, we need to see "the fear of the LORD" as, in some way, a gift from God.

Defining Our Terms

Question 94 of the Heidelberg Catechism asks, "What does the Lord require in the first commandment?" Part of the answer reads, "That I rightly know the only true God, trust him alone, and look to God for every good thing humbly and patiently, *and love, fear, and honor God with all my heart*. In short, that I give up anything rather than go against God's will in any way."[2]

Focusing on one aspect of the answer, notice that our duty is to "fear" God with all our hearts. Zacharius Ursinus, one of the authors of the catechism, provides a valuable description of fear in his commentary on this very question. It is worthwhile to carefully reflect on his explanation. He begins with a broad definition:

> The fear of God is to acknowledge his infinite wrath against sin, his power to punish it, and to regard an offence against God, accompanied with aversion to him, the greatest evil, and for this reason to hate and detest sin; and to be willing to suffer all other things sooner than offend God in the smallest matter. Or it is an unwillingness to offend God, resulting from submission

2 Heidelberg Catechism, https://www.crcna.org/ (emphasis added).

> to God and a knowledge of his wisdom, power, justice, and the right which he has over all creatures.[3]

His definition raises the objection that something good—in fact, the highest good—should not be something we fear. His response leads him to reflect on the distinctions between love and fear. Love follows after good and desires to be united to God; fear turns away from evil and dreads separation from God. Love arises from knowing the goodness of God; fear comes from knowing his power and justice and his rights over all creatures. From here, Ursinus describes what fear is for the Christian specifically and, in doing so, weaves together both love and fear:

> The fear of God which is in the regenerate in this life is an acknowledgment of sin and the wrath of God, and a sincere sorrow arising from a view of the sins we have committed, from the offence we have offered God by our sins, and from the miseries we and others endure in consequence of sin, accompanied with a fear of future sins and punishment, and an ardent desire to escape these evils, by reason of the knowledge of the mercy of God made known to us in Christ.

His definition becomes increasingly personal. There is "sincere sorrow" and a recognition that God's mercy in Christ is trampled on by our sin. Yet he goes a step further, describing fear in familial terms as "filial fear." It is called this, he writes,

3 The following quotes are from Zacharias Ursinus, *Commentary on the Heidelberg Catechism*, trans. G. W. Williard (Netherlands Reformed, 2015), 513–14.

> because it is such as children cherish towards their parents, who are sorry on account of a father's anger and displeasure, and fear lest they should again offend him and be punished; and are, nevertheless, continually assured of the love, and good will of the father towards them. Hence they love him, and are more deeply grieved on account of the love which they cherish towards him, whom they have offended.

Christian fear cannot be properly grasped without its wonderful connection to love. This leads Ursinus to address the difference between good fear and bad fear, "filial fear" and "servile fear." Filial fear arises out of confidence in God and love for him, hates sin and hates offending God, and is bound up with the certainty of salvation and eternal life. Servile fear, on the contrary, doesn't arise from faith and has no desire for change. It arises from a sense of displeasure in God; it hates the punishment for sin, not sin itself; it flees from God; and it doubts the grace and mercy of God, living in dread of eternal punishment. Zero fear leads to license; servile fear leads to despair.

Product or Manufacturer?

Fear is loving reverence for God. It is the ongoing acknowledgment of God's status as creator, redeemer, and judge. In Psalm 119, as elsewhere in Scripture, the "fear of the Lord" is given a fairly straightforward definition. The psalmist writes,

> I am a companion of all who fear you,
> of those who keep your precepts. (Ps. 119:63)

Those who fear the Lord are synonymous with those who keep the law of Yahweh. This fear is neither a slavish nor servile fear, as we saw above. It is a fear and obedience rooted in covenantal love: God's love for us and our loving response to his fatherly care. If we want to know what it means to walk in the fear of the Lord, look no further than his commands.

Earlier on, the psalmist makes another connection between fear and God's word:

> Confirm to your servant your promise,
> that you may be feared. (119:38)

God's words of promise that we encounter in Scripture produce fear in us as he fulfills those promises. As one commentator puts it, "By doing what he has promised to do for his servant, the Lord will prompt the psalmist afresh to revere him, as he demonstrates anew that he can be trusted."[4] God's speech—in this case, his promises—engenders fear. The fear of the Lord is the product; God, through his word, is the manufacturer of that fear.

There is an odd but repeated experience I have every time I read Psalm 19. It happens when I come to that famous section where the psalmist begins to extol God's law, and I get the feeling of rapture and delight:

> The law of the LORD is perfect, . . .
> the testimony of the LORD is sure, . . .
> the precepts of the LORD are right, . . .
> the commandment of the LORD is pure. (Ps. 19:7–8)

4 Daniel J. Estes, *Psalms 73–150*, The New American Commentary (B&H, 2019), 411.

Then I encounter, "The *fear* of the LORD is clean" (19:9), and that's when my mind hits the brakes. It seems like someone just crashed the party. The psalmist praises God's word for its many-splendored beauty, using a range of terms—law, testimony, precepts, commandments—but then inserts what seems like an oddball into the mix: fear. The fear of the Lord, as we have seen, is most often treated as one's posture or attitude toward God. That is how many commentators understand its use in this psalm. If that is what the psalmist has in mind here, then fear really is the misfit of Psalm 19. Given how every other term in the passage is a clear synonym for the law, however, it would seem that the fear of the Lord is another term for the law itself. Since the law is the very thing that teaches and produces fear, it is so closely associated as to be described as the "fear of the LORD." This simply points to the intimate connection between instruction regarding fearing God and the production of that fear. We cannot fear (attitude) without "the fear" (the law or teaching).

The Goodness of Fear

Understanding what the fear of the Lord is, we can now return to the question of how fear might be a gift. If the fear of the Lord is wedded to a deep love for God and is expressed as a real sorrow for sinning against our Lord and friend, it is clear that this fear must be a gift. This kind of posture toward God is never self-generated. In fact, this is why Ursinus describes this fear as belonging to the "regenerate in this life"—that is, those who have been born again by God. The fear of God is a gift in the sense that it is just an expression of the new life granted to us by God, the giver of life.

Fear is a gift in another sense. The book of Proverbs regularly points to the benefits that come to those who fear the Lord. They receive wisdom (Prov. 9:10), life (10:27; 14:27; 19:23), confidence in God's protection (14:26), riches and honor (22:4), and blessedness (28:14). Fear is a gift that gives gifts. Several studies point to the connection between our sense of awe and our well-being. Those who have had experiences of awe—of nature or of anything seemingly transcendent—demonstrate greater humility, less stress, greater life satisfaction, and even immune health.[5] Fear is good for us, and God knows this. That's why he gives us the gift of his word to produce the gift of fear and, in doing so, opens the door to a world of treasures.

Thrice happy man who fears the Lord,
Loves his commands, and trusts his word;
Honor and peace his days attend,
And blessings to his seed descend.

His soul, well fixed upon the Lord,
Draws heav'nly courage from his word;
Amidst the darkness light shall rise,
To cheer his heart and bless his eyes.

ISAAC WATTS
"Thrice Happy Man Who Fears the Lord"
1740

5 Reeves, *Rejoice and Tremble*, 81–82.

6

The Gift of Salvation

My soul longs for your salvation;
I hope in your word. . . .

I am yours; save me,
for I have sought your precepts. . . .

Salvation is far from the wicked,
for they do not seek your statutes.

PSALM 119:81, 94, 155

WHEN SALVATION IS SPOKEN OF in Scripture, it often refers to something very earthly. Enemies assail, atrocities abound, and natural disasters wreak havoc. What does *salvation* mean in these circumstances? Think deliverance, rescue, or liberation. If famine has ravaged the land, relief through the provision of food *is* salvation. If enemies are persecuting God's people, their end or the rescue of the faithful—these *are* salvation. This kind of thinking pervades the

Old Testament. Yet it is not solely an Old Testament thing. In Luke's recounting of Jesus's birth story, Zechariah prophesies about the salvation that the Christ will bring, and his prophecy has a very earthly frame of reference. Notice all the occurrences of *redemption*, *deliverance*, and *salvation*, but also notice what he points to as salvation:

> Blessed be the Lord God of Israel,
>   for he has visited and *redeemed* his people
> and has raised up a horn of *salvation* for us
>   in the house of his servant David,
> as he spoke by the mouth of his holy prophets from of old,
> that we should be *saved* from our enemies
>   and from the hand of all who hate us;
> to show the mercy promised to our fathers
>   and to remember his holy covenant,
> the oath that he swore to our father Abraham, to grant us
>   that we, being *delivered* from the hand of our enemies,
> might serve him without fear,
>   in holiness and righteousness before him all our days.
>   (Luke 1:68–75)

In the person of the Messiah, God has redeemed his people by saving them from their enemies and from the hands of all who hate them. Certainly, we could interpret Zechariah as speaking about deliverance from Satan, our enemy, but he surely has very human enemies in mind. So even when God's people talk about the Messiah's work of salvation, they think in earthly terms, as well as spiritual.

Why does this matter, especially when we know that salvation involves far more than just the alleviation of difficult circumstances? It brings into sharper focus the connection our psalm makes between salvation and God's word. The connection is direct, and that's where the interesting stuff begins.

Hope and Seek

The psalmist cries out for salvation in our verses. And his confidence that his appeal will be answered relates closely to the way he is oriented to God's word:

> My soul longs for salvation;
> I hope in your word. (Ps. 119:81)

His hope rests on God's promises of favor, and so he trusts that the salvation he longs for will be carried out. The connection is even clearer in our other two passages. There is a contrast between two kinds of people—the righteous and the wicked—but the connection between Scripture and salvation is undeniable for both. In the case of the righteous,

> I am yours; save me,
> for *I have sought* your precepts. (119:94)

As for the wicked,

> Salvation is far from the wicked,
> for *they do not seek* your statutes. (119:155)

The key in both cases involves *seeking*. Those who are saved are those who seek God's precepts and statutes.

Except for when that's not the case. When salvation is seen in earthly terms, it raises problems for the connection between salvation and God's word. Experience tells us that it is not always the case that God's people are delivered from hardship, persecution, and trial simply because they seek God's word. In fact, keeping God's word may be the very reason their hardships persist. In a sermon on Psalm 119:155, the Puritan Thomas Manton faces this problem head-on. He first lays out the issue through the voice of the preacher in Ecclesiastes, who writes,

> It is the same for all, since the same event happens to the righteous and the wicked, to the good and the evil, to the clean and the unclean, to him who sacrifices and him who does not sacrifice. As the good one is, so is the sinner, and he who swears is as he who shuns an oath. (Eccl. 9:2)

Then Manton comments,

> We see . . . that those outward things are given indifferently to good and bad, and the wicked are as free from temporal punishment as others, and enjoy all prosperity in this world, even sometimes to the envy and offence of God's children, and the hardening of their own hearts; and, which is more, that often it happeneth to the just according to the work of the wicked, and to the wicked according to the work of the righteous (Eccles 8:14); that is, evil to good men, and good to evil men. As to outward things, the advantage is usually on the side of the worst.[1]

1 The following quotes are from Thomas Manton, "Sermon 173," in *The Complete Works of Thomas Manton*, 22 vols. (J. Nisbet, 1870–1875), 9:147–48.

In this sermon, which is intended to convince his audience of the truth of our verse—that temporal salvation, as well as eternal salvation, is far from the wicked—Manton concedes that there is a certain measure of difficulty here. "We must grant what is to be granted," he writes. Part of his solution to the problem involves acknowledging that "temporal things not being absolutely good or evil, the Lord taketh a liberty in the dispensation of them." The key is the phrase "absolutely good or evil." Manton suggests that since the alleviation of hardship (i.e., earthly salvation) is not absolutely, without a shadow of a doubt, good for us, there is some mystery regarding whether God will or will not grant that temporal salvation. Only God knows what is ultimately good for us, and he "takes a liberty" in granting those earthly experiences of salvation. Eternal salvation, however, since it is absolutely and ultimately good, is never executed with this apparent inconsistency and mystery. It is guaranteed. Pulling it all together, Manton concludes,

> None that live godly can fail of the eternal promises; none that goeth on still in his trespasses can escape the eternal threatenings. But the temporal promises and threatenings, being of things not simply good and evil, are not so absolutely fixed, but God will take a liberty sometimes to cross his hands, out of his general indulgence to give prosperity to the wicked, and out of his fatherly wisdom to chasten the godly; and so all things come alike to all.

So let's return to our theme. How does all this relate to seeking God's word? What Manton suggests is that those who seek God's word—that is, the godly—will never fail to receive the promises of eternal salvation. This seems pretty straightforward for those well versed in the gospel. The gospel is that word we believe, hold on to, hope in, and seek, and it connects us to everlasting life—as long as we continue to believe. The word is the good seed planted that bears fruit, the most important of which is eternal life. We are confident that everyone who calls on the name of the Lord will be saved, and that calling on the Lord is dependent upon hearing his words (Rom. 10:13–15). As Christians, it should not take much to persuade us that the word of God has the power to save us, and that we can be secure in that belief.

What, then, of the problem of temporal salvation? Though it is true that the righteous are not always rescued from their earthly travails, we must remember at least three things to help us make sense of this difficulty. First, the difference between the righteous and unrighteous is that salvation is promised to one and not the other. Therefore, when an evil person is rescued or finds himself in comfort, it is not an expression of covenantal love but possibly of the Lord's judgment or discipline. In Manton's words,

> Salvation is far from the wicked, because they cannot lay claim to God's favourable providence, or look for the continuance of it with any confidence, because they have no right, no promise to build upon. The word of God speaketh no good to them, whatever God may do out of his general indulgence.

Second, in light of this, the righteous can and should have more confidence that God is able to deliver them from their earthly troubles. While God does not always rescue, he is more likely to rescue and give justice to his faithful ones.

Third, even when we get no temporal relief, the promise of God is that we will ultimately, without fail, receive salvation from our earthly trials in eternity. Salvation, in the final analysis, is really deliverance from earthly troubles, not just final judgment and the fires of hell. And because eternal life is not some transport to some other realm or atemporal reality but a continuation of this life, we will receive salvation within this same timeline and history.

Back to the Word

The answers to these theological and existential questions aren't simple, but the word of God is sure. Lest we get lost in the weeds of a theological difficulty, we must remember that the psalmist's song is in praise of a God who is faithful to his word of promise *and* in praise of a word of promise that connects us to a faithful God. This is where Manton ends a sermon on one of our other verses (Ps. 119:81). Speaking specifically about the role of the word of God in producing hope for salvation, he offers two helpful points.

First, he reminds us that the word of God is "the law of commerce between us and God":

> In the promissory part it showeth what salvation and deliverance we may expect from him; and in the mandatory part, upon what terms, and who are the persons qualified to receive this deliverance: and without heeding of these things, hope is a groundless presumption, as if we expect things not promised,

> or not in the way wherein they are promised. We must have an eye both on the promises and the precepts—the one to encourage us, the other to direct us.[2]

Without the word, we do not know what to expect or hope for. And if we don't hope for and expect something, we are less likely to pray for it and receive it.

Second, Manton reminds us that the best way to hold on to God is by his word. He writes, "Whatever his dispensations [providence] be, though he withhold comfort and deliverance from us, yet it [i.e., his providence] will do well in time. Therefore, whether he smileth or frowneth, his word should be our support. His dispensations vary, but his word is firm."

Praise God for the great salvation(s) he's given us through his word!

How precious is the book divine,
By inspiration giv'n;
Bright as a lamp its pages shine
To guide our souls to Heav'n.

Its light descending from above,
Our gloomy world to cheer,
Displays a Savior's boundless love,
And brings His glories near.

2 The following quotes are from Thomas Manton, "Sermon 89," in *Complete Works*, 7:360.

It shows to man his wand'ring ways,
And where his feet have trod;
And brings to view the matchless grace
Of a forgiving God.

O'er all the straight and narrow way
Its radiant beams are cast;
A light whose never weary ray
Grows brightest at the last.

It sweetly cheers our fainting hearts
In this dark vale of tears;
Life, light and joy it still imparts,
And quells our rising fears.

This lamp, through all the tedious night
Of life, shall guide our way,
Till we behold the clearer light
Of an eternal day.

JOHN FAWCETT
"How Precious Is the Book Divine"
1782

7

The Gift of Fruitfulness

But his delight is in the law of the Lord,
and on his law he meditates day and night.

He is like a tree
planted by streams of water
that yields its fruit in its season,
and its leaf does not wither.
In all that he does, he prospers.

PSALM 1:2–3

IT IS AMAZING how much the Bible talks about fruit. It speaks about it literally and metaphorically, positively and negatively. It is obsessed with fruit, especially as a way of describing our spiritual lives. We are meant to bear fruit. We are called to live fruitful lives. In fact, the Bible begins with the mandate, "Be fruitful and multiply" (Gen. 1:28). At the very core of who we are—not just as Christians but as humans made in God's image—is the call to be fruitful.

American author Annie Dillard, in her award-winning *Pilgrim at Tinker Creek*, marveled at the fruitfulness of the tulip tree. She reflects,

> There's a real power here. It is amazing that trees can turn gravel and bitter salts into these soft-lipped lobes, as if I were to bite down on a granite slab and start to swell, bud, and flower. Trees seem to do their feats so effortlessly. Every year a given tree creates absolutely from scratch ninety-nine percent of its living parts. Water lifting up tree trunks can climb one hundred and fifty feet an hour; in full summer a tree can, and does, heave a ton of water every day. A big elm in a single season might make as many as six million leaves, wholly intricate, without budging an inch; I couldn't make one.[1]

This is not a cool, detached reflection on a biological process. This is an expression of longing for the kind of explosive fruitfulness that one witnesses taking place in a tulip tree. She observes, with awe, an invisible power working in unspectacular ways to produce spectacular beauty and abundance. This is a metaphor for the Christian life—at least, the kind of life we should long for.

Most times, when I read the parable of the sower (Matt. 13:1–23; Mark 4:1–20; Luke 8:4–15), I tend to focus on the question "What type of soil am I?" This is probably the right thing to focus on, but I often don't zero in on the good soil beyond recognizing that it is good, unlike the other three bad soils. I'm alert to the goodness of the soil but not on the result of that

1 Annie Dillard, *Pilgrim at Tinker Creek* (HarperPerennial, 1974), 112.

goodness. What does Jesus say about this soil? "But those that were sown on the good soil are the ones who hear the word and accept it and bear fruit, thirtyfold and sixtyfold and a hundredfold" (Mark 4:20). Or, "As for that in the good soil, they are those who, hearing the word, hold it fast in an honest and good heart, and bear fruit with patience" (Luke 8:15). The good soil—that is, those who "hear the word and accept it" and, upon hearing it, "hold it fast in an honest and good heart"—experience the kind of explosive fruitfulness Dillard observed.

Imagine one small seed yielding thirty, sixty, and even a hundred times what was planted. In fact, perhaps more important than the soil is the seed planted in that soil. Jesus makes clear that the seed is the word of God. There is a real generative power in the seed, an untapped potency that, in the proper environment, produces a harvest. What is clear from the parable is that Jesus intends his word to produce abundant fruit in his people. What is the fruit that the word produces?

Fruit of the Spirit

The easiest place to start in thinking about fruit is Paul's famous list in Galatians: "But the fruit of the Spirit is love, joy, peace, patience, kindness, goodness, faithfulness, gentleness, self-control" (Gal. 5:22–23). Rather than speaking of "works" of the Spirit (as Paul speaks of "works of the flesh" in 5:19), the apostle calls the virtues "fruit." Jonathan Edwards views the fruit as the inner attitudes of the heart toward God:

> The Word of God makes those that understand it to be of holy dispositions and affections, to have holy desires and motions of

> heart that are acceptable unto God: the exercises of love to God and longing desires after him, the exercise of delight in Jesus Christ, the exercises of submission to the will of God, thankfulness for mercies, the exercise of a penitent spirit in mourning for sin and humbling himself before God for it, longing desires after holiness and after more communion with God, the exercises of faith, of dependence upon God and a fiducial committing ourselves to him, that inward worship and devotion that a pious soul often exercises. Such fruits as these, though appearing in no external action, are yet precious fruits of righteousness and such as will be rewarded.[2]

The fruit of the Spirit is essentially a heart that loves and delights in God. But notice that Edwards views the word of God as that which brings forth this fruit of a transformed heart. The Spirit of God and the word of God belong together as sower (and fertilizer?) and seed.

Calvin, on the other hand, sees the fruit as others-oriented behaviors. He writes,

> *Joy* does not here, I think, denote that "joy in the Holy Ghost" (Romans 14:17), of which he speaks elsewhere, but that cheerful behavior towards our fellow-men which is the opposite of moroseness. *Faith* means truth, and is contrasted with cunning, deceit, and falsehood, as *peace* is with quarrels and contentions. *Long-suffering* is gentleness of mind, which disposes us to take everything in good part, and not to be easily offended. The

2 Jonathan Edwards, *Profitable Hearers of the Word*, in *Sermons and Discourses: 1723–1729*, ed. Kenneth P. Minkema, vol. 14 of *The Works of Jonathan Edwards* (Yale University Press, 1997), 258.

> other terms require no explanation, for the dispositions of the mind must be learned from the outward conduct.[3]

Here, the fruit has to do with how we interact with others. The Spirit uses Scripture to make us cheerful, not contentious nor easily offended. The Spirit works through God's word to produce a harvest of holy attitudes *and* holy actions.

Vine and Branches

The mission statement of a campus ministry I was involved in before and after college focused on evangelizing and preparing students for world-changing ministry. We were passionate about fulfilling the Great Commission (Matt. 28:18–20). We regularly walked around campus talking to students about Christ, held debates on faith issues like whether God exists, and sent out scores of students around the world on short-term and long-term mission trips. Our heartbeat was to be God's agents in helping people come to know Christ. During that time, when I heard someone teach on Jesus's words "I am the vine; you are the branches. Whoever abides in me and I in him, he it is that bears much fruit" (John 15:5), it was often understood that *fruit* meant more people coming to Christ. Yet, while I really wanted to see more and more people's lives changed, I always questioned if that was exactly what Jesus meant in this passage.

At the beginning of this passage, Jesus makes it clear that bearing fruit is of utmost importance to the Father. Every branch that doesn't bear fruit is cut off and burned; the branches that bear fruit are pruned so that they can bear even more fruit (15:2). Jesus's words are the

3 John Calvin, *Commentaries on the Epistles of Paul to the Galatians and Ephesians*, trans. William Pringle, in *Calvin's Commentaries* (Baker, 2003), 167–68 (emphasis original).

Father's instrument for pruning us (15:3). But the key to bearing fruit is *abiding* in Christ, who is the life-giving vine to which the branches are attached. Jesus explains an important truth about abiding when he replaces "Whoever abides in me and I in him" (15:5) with "If you abide in me, and *my words* abide in you" (15:7). Abiding centers on Christ's words residing in our hearts. Jesus also specifies that abiding in him is abiding in his love (15:9). What is it to abide in his love? Jesus says, "If you keep my commandments, you will abide in my love" (15:10). Abiding in Christ and his love means receiving his word and keeping it because we belong to him. In other words, Christ *and* his word are the secret powers working inside each branch so that it produces a harvest—in this case, a harvest of joy (15:11), intimacy with Christ (15:12–15), and answered prayer (15:16).

Delighted Meditation

On some level, the Lord's teaching, as well as Paul's, is a reflection on and application of Psalm 1. According to the psalmist, those who bear fruit possess two main characteristics: they delight in the law of the Lord and, because of this delight, meditate on it day and night. Those who delight in the law do not see it as a form of drudgery by which to live. They know that God's instruction is good for them, so they joyfully submit to it. And because they delight in the law, they meditate on it continuously. Describing meditation, one commentator writes,

> "Meditating" suggests the murmur of recitation; the scroll is read, or passages are recited from memory, all in a kind of intoned way, and mingled with formulas of praise and prayer, sounding especially the names of the Lord. It is because this "meditation" is a communion

> with the Lord that, ideally, it would be continued day and night. And for the same reason, it is not an irksome labour, but the highest delight. And again for the same reason, it is indeed fruitful.[4]

The blessed person is not a drive-thru consumer of Scripture. Instead, they memorize it; they chew on it. And the result is spiritual vibrancy and fruitfulness. The fruitfulness described here is comprehensive. The psalmist says that those who love God's law are like trees whose roots go deep into the richest of soils. They are alive. They are resilient, and their leaves don't wither during seasons of drought. This does not mean that they experience no hardship but that they regularly display the signs of God's blessing and fullness in their lives. *Everything* they do prospers. In every sphere of life, there is abundance. Is this not what we all long for?

The "real power"—to borrow Dillard's phrase—behind this kind of life is God himself working through his word, or better, God working in the one who delights in his word.

> Oh, precious Jesus—may I be no longer unfruitful in your garden!
>
> Lord, do as you have said. Dig around me, and pour on me all the sweet influences of your Holy Spirit—which, like the rain, the sun, and the dew of heaven, may cause me to bring forth fruit to God.[5]

---

4 J. H. Eaton, *The Psalms: A Historical and Spiritual Commentary with an Introduction and New Translation* (Continuum, 2008), 62.

5 Richard Hawker, quoted in Robert Elmer, ed., *Piercing Heaven: Prayers of the Puritans* (Lexham, 2019), 37.

Almighty God, your Word is cast
like seed into the ground;
now let the dew of heav'n descend
and righteous fruits abound.

Let not the foe of Christ and man
this holy seed remove,
but give it root in ev'ry heart
to bring forth fruits of love.

Let not the world's deceitful cares
the rising plant destroy,
but let it yield a hundredfold
the fruits of peace and joy.

Whene'er the precious seed is sown,
life-giving grace bestow
that all whose souls the truth receive
its saving pow'r may know.

JOHN CAWOOD
"Almighty God, Thy Word Is Cast"
1819

8

The Gift of Warnings

Moreover, by them is your servant warned;
in keeping them there is great reward.

PSALM 19:11

"I KNOW, I KNOW" has to be one of the most common phrases heard in our home. It is a fairly typical response from the younger members of the family toward elder members who caution them about the potential consequences of their poor behavior. It may also be the response to something as benign as, "Be careful, or you might get hurt." Regardless of what lies behind the somewhat dismissive "I know, I know," it is clear that the warning is not seen as a gift. An annoyance? Yes. But a gift? Hardly. Yet in our more sober moments, we know that warning signs are an enormous grace. We see this in a number of areas in our lives.

If I am driving on a mountain road in a rainstorm and, through my foggy windshield, see a sign that says, "Bridge Out," I would certainly not be dismissive of the caution. Traveling at thirty miles an hour, barely able to see twenty feet in front of me, I would be grateful for the warning sign. It might save my life. Think about tornado sirens and fire alarms. They are advance warning systems designed to help prepare for and, hopefully, avoid the worst. Warnings are gifts to those who have ears to hear.

God of All Caution

As much as we may believe that our parents are the most cautious, warning-obsessed people imaginable, it would be difficult for them to top God in this department. The Lord cries out to his people:

> Hear, O my people, while I admonish you!
> O Israel, if you would but listen to me! (Ps. 81:8)

Through the voice of Wisdom, he warns,

> Because you have ignored all my counsel
> and would have none of my reproof,
> I also will laugh at your calamity;
> I will mock when terror strikes you,
> when terror strikes you like a storm
> and your calamity comes like a whirlwind,
> when distress and anguish come upon you.
> (Prov. 1:25–27)

Over and over again, he warns. The apostle Paul calls the Father "the God of all comfort," and this is a fitting description of a God who kindly and gently "comforts us in all our affliction"

(2 Cor. 1:3–4). But it is equally fitting to describe God as "the God of all caution," who cautions us so that we do not experience unnecessary affliction. Both comfort and caution are expressions of God's steadfast love.

A Big Book of Warnings

While it is probably not the best way to describe it, the Bible can be fairly characterized as a big book of warnings. Think about it. Many of God's conditional promises in the early books of the Bible are warnings (e.g., Gen. 2:16–17; Ex. 23:20–33; Deut. 28:1–68). If you obey, you will be blessed. But beware: If you don't obey, you will experience the curses of the covenant, death, stoning, and so forth. Even the history of the monarchy (1 Samuel through 2 Chronicles) is a long cautionary tale with the same message: Do not be unfaithful like Israel and its kings. Proverbs and Ecclesiastes are full of warnings. And then comes a whole genre devoted to warnings: the Prophets. This is the Bible as we know it—a book filled with dozens upon dozens of cautions, threats, and admonitions, graciously given because of our proneness to wander.

This is precisely the note that our passage from Psalm 19 is striking. The psalmist praises the word of God for its many benefits and attributes. It revives the soul, makes the simple wise. It rejoices the heart and enlightens the eyes. It endures forever and is altogether righteous, more valuable than gold, and sweeter than honey (Ps. 19:7–10). Yet included in this list, maybe even as the culmination of the list, is the psalmist's praise for God's commands because "by them is your servant warned" (19:11). Warnings should not be seen as something merely tolerated, an annoyance, or an unfortunate intrusion in an otherwise pleasant song about God's law. Warnings are something to sing about.

It is astonishing the range of warnings the psalmists sing about. You don't get very far in the Psalter before you encounter one:

> Now therefore, O kings, be wise;
> be warned, O rulers of the earth.
> Serve the LORD with fear,
> and rejoice with trembling.
> Kiss the Son,
> lest he be angry, and you perish in the way,
> for his wrath is quickly kindled. (Ps. 2:10–12)

The kings of the nations are warned that their rebellion against God and his anointed one will only bring ruin. A few psalms later, the hardhearted are warned,

> If a man does not repent, God will whet his sword;
> he has bent and readied his bow;
> he has prepared for him his deadly weapons,
> making his arrows fiery shafts. (7:12–13)

Then we have Psalm 95, with its seemingly dissonant notes of joy and deathly serious caution. It begins,

> Oh come, let us sing to the LORD;
> let us make a joyful noise to the rock of our
> salvation! (95:1)

It continues along this joyful path of thanking God and recounting his great works of creation and redemption, through almost seven verses. Then it takes what seems like an abrupt turn, and now, God addresses the reader or hearer directly:

> Today, if *you* hear his voice,
> do not harden your hearts. (95:7–8)

Then a different kind of recounting occurs. Rather than reciting God's acts of faithful love, God recounts Israel's acts of faithless rebellion in the wilderness (95:8–9). Their waywardness persisted during the whole course of their wilderness wanderings, inciting God to say in the penultimate verse, "For forty years I loathed that generation" (95:10). But the full force of the warning is not felt until we come to the final verse, where God specifies the grave consequences of their rebellion (and, presumably, of *all* rebellion):

> Therefore I swore in my wrath,
> "They shall not enter my rest." (95:11)

There is no mistaking that this is a song of praise. But does the praise end at 95:7, before the warning? Is God's character being extolled only in the happy verses? The one who warns is the God who is King (95:3), Maker (95:6), *and* shepherd (95:7). The warning issued overflows from a shepherd's heart. The Lord is pulling out all the stops not only for the wilderness generation about whom the psalm is written but also for future generations. *We* are being warned by God, as is evident in the book of Hebrews' adapting the passage for its own purposes of warning its hearers (Heb. 3:7–11). The God of the Old and New Testaments warns from a heart of concern, and he does it through his written word.

A Word About Conviction

I've often heard people speak about "feeling convicted" or say that the Spirit convicted them about something. This is probably shorthand for their sense that they are doing something worthy of repentance and change. This feeling of conviction can sometimes feel like it comes from nowhere, just out of the blue. While this may be the case at times, I wonder if conviction really is that contextless. What I mean is this: I suspect that the context for our sense of conviction—the reason we are alert to it—is a conscience informed by God's word.

Peter's Pentecost sermon in Acts 2 is an apt illustration. We tend to think of his message as a kind of "gospel" sermon, especially given the positive response of the crowd. It is, however, also appropriate to see the sermon as an extended warning. The sermon begins, of all things, with an accusation: "Men of Israel, hear these words: Jesus of Nazareth, a man attested to you by God . . . *you* crucified and killed by the hands lawless men" (Acts 2:22–23). The "day of the Lord" has come (2:20), and they welcomed it by killing the one who brings God's end time blessings. Yet their wickedness was not the final word. God raised Jesus from the dead and, through him, poured out the powerful manifestation of the Spirit that all experienced that day (2:24–35).

He then sums up his message but not without a final accusation: "Let all the house of Israel therefore know for certain that God has made him both Lord and Christ, this Jesus *whom you crucified*" (2:36). At this point, the mood changes. The passage reads, "Now when they heard *this* they were cut to the heart" (2:37). They were "cut to the heart"—convicted—by Peter's message. What is "this" that they were convicted by? While it potentially refers to Peter's whole sermon, the most immediate reference is to the accusation, "You killed the Messiah." Being cut to the heart, they ask the apostles what they need to do to avoid what was implicitly threatened and receive the gift implicitly offered in Peter's message. He responds that they need to repent and be identified with Christ (2:38). And as if the warning dimension of the message was unclear, Peter "continued to exhort them" with explicit warnings like, "Save yourselves from this crooked generation" (2:40).

In fact, this pattern is repeated in many, if not all, of the sermons in Acts.[1] After healing the lame man (3:7) and drawing a lot of attention to themselves, Peter preaches another sermon that begins on a similar note. He lays out the charges against them, saying, "The God of Abraham . . . glorified his servant Jesus, whom you delivered over and denied in the presence of Pilate, when he had decided to release him. But you denied the Holy and righteous One . . . and you killed the Author of life" (3:13–15). After this, he pleads, "Repent therefore, and turn back, that your sins may be blotted out" (3:19). The implication is that their sins remained on them as long as they were estranged from Christ. Then Peter finally makes his warning explicit, claiming that everyone who does not listen to Christ (and his messengers) "shall be destroyed from the people" (3:23). This gospel sermon is met with similar

1 See also Acts 10 and 13. I am indebted to Howard Spencer for making me aware of this pattern elsewhere in Acts.

results as the one in the previous chapter: "Many of those who had heard the word believed, and the number of the men came to about five thousand" (4:4). Peter's sermons are evidence that good news and accusation, gospel and warning, go hand-in-hand and both, taken together, produce profound results.

The point for us is this: Conviction does not typically happen in a vacuum. Rather, it comes to those who hear and embrace the warnings of Scripture. A general principle we may safely assume is that the more we are warned, the more we are convicted; and with more conviction, there is more obedience; and more obedience leads to greater blessing. To put it simply, the goodness of God is expressed in the gift of his words of warning.

Spirit blest, who art adored,
With the Father and the Word,
One Eternal God and Lord:
Hear us Holy Spirit.

Spirit, showing us the way,
Warning when we go astray,
Pleading in us when we pray:
Hear us Holy Spirit.

Spirit, whom our failings grieve,
Whom the world will not receive,
Who dost help us to believe:
Hear us Holy Spirit.

Spirit, aiding all who yearn
More of truth Divine to learn,
And with deeper love to burn:
Hear us Holy Spirit.
Amen.

THOMAS BENSON POLLOCK
"Spirit Blest, Who Art Adored"
1871

9

The Gift of Peace

Great peace have those who love your law;
nothing can make them stumble.

PSALM 119:165

THERE IS A WONDERFUL SCENE in the 2000 comedy *Miss Congeniality* where contestants at a beauty pageant are asked the all-important question: "What is the one most important thing our society needs?" One contestant steps forward and answers, "World peace." Then the next: "World peace." Contestant after contestant, the same refrain: "World peace." Then the lead character (an undercover police officer) takes her turn. The host repeats the question, and she responds, "That there would be harsher punishments for parole violators, Stan." The crowd and host are stunned silent. Then recognizing that this was probably not going to win her the beauty contest, she immediately alters her answer and adds, ". . . and world peace." The crowd, now satisfied, erupts in applause.

If someone were to ask Jesus, "What is the one most important thing your disciples will need after you depart?" perhaps his answer would not be too far from these beauty pageant contestants. Toward the end of Jesus's earthly ministry, he promises his disciples, "Peace I leave with you; my peace I give to you. Not as the world gives do I give to you. Let not your hearts be troubled, neither let them be afraid" (John 14:27). He makes sure to leave them with something that will transcend their circumstances and root them for when things get difficult. While beauty pageant contestants may be unclear about what world peace entails, Jesus is quite clear about what peace is all about and why it is so important to leave with his disciples.

The biblical notion of peace is quite all-encompassing. According to one scholar, "It is more than absence of warfare and hostility. It is a state of positive friendship and security between two parties, often the result of restitution and reconciliation."[1] Peace not only speaks primarily of a restored relationship to God but also about well-functioning relationships with others (e.g. Rom. 5:1; 14:19). Peace, or the Hebrew *shalom*, often refers to well-being, prosperity, and satisfaction in life.[2] But the word also has an internal, perhaps psychological dimension to it, as when Paul says, "And the peace of God, which surpasses all understanding, will guard your hearts and your minds in Christ Jesus" (Phil. 4:7), and "Let the peace of Christ rule in your hearts" (Col. 3:15). And relevant to Jesus's promise, peace

1 P. A. Barker, "Rest, Peace," in *Dictionary of the Old Testament: Pentateuch*, ed. T. Desmond Alexander and David W. Barker (IVP Academic, 2003), 690.

2 Daniel J. Estes, *Psalms 73–150*, in The New American Commentary (B&H, 2019), 437.

is a feature of righteous kingly rule and of the messianic age. As the royal Messiah, Jesus promises peace in the form of his ongoing kingly presence and kingly rule in the world and among his people.[3] Therefore, there are external dimensions of peace (e.g., relational health, material well-being, and the messianic age) that result in internal peace (e.g., the absence of troubled hearts and fear) (John 14:27).

Grace and Peace to You

The most obvious thing about peace is its source. There is a bumper sticker that says, "No Jesus, no peace; know Jesus, know peace." While it's perhaps somewhat corny, as most bumper stickers tend to be, it does convey the most basic of biblical truths about peace. This truth is captured in Paul's greetings to the churches, which follow an identical pattern: "Grace to you and peace from God our Father and the Lord Jesus Christ" (1 Cor. 1:3; 2 Cor. 1:2; Gal. 1:3; Eph. 1:2; Phil. 1:2).

Every aspect of peace comes from the hand of the triune God. It is the gift of God the Father. It is also the gift of the Son. Paul writes, "Now may the Lord of peace himself give you peace at all times in every way" (2 Thess. 3:16). It is also among the fruit of the Spirit (Gal. 5:22–23). Peace—that sense of wholeness, well-being, relational health, inner tranquility—is an overflow of God's own being. What God pours out on us is an expression of his own life as God. The only way to have peace is to enter into communion with God and to nurture that communion with him. To know God is to know peace.

3 Marianne Meye Thompson, *John: A Commentary* (Westminster John Knox, 2015), 316–17.

Yet in Scripture, the experience of peace, externally and internally, is connected to words: words spoken, words read, words received. For example, in the blessing that Aaron and his sons pronounced on the people of Israel, we find the words "The LORD bless you . . . and give you peace" (Num. 6:24–26). Pronouncing a blessing lies somewhere between an incantation and a typical prayer. It is a pronouncement that is meant to assure the people of the Lord's promises and to strengthen their confidence that his care would follow them into their day-to-day lives. When the blessing is uttered repeatedly over them, God bestows peace on them not because the blessing is a magic formula but because the gracious God chooses to act according to his own promise carried in the blessing.

Most importantly, peace *with God* comes through our response to words. Paul calls the good news the "gospel of peace" (Eph. 6:15). The Puritan William Gurnall comments on how and why the gospel brings peace:

> The gospel, published and preached, is the great instrument of God to effect this peace. Before peace be concluded between God and the creature, both must be agreed; as God to pardon, so the sinner to accept and embrace peace upon God's own terms: but how shall this be done? The heart of man is so deeply rooted in its enmity against God, that it requires a strength to pluck up this, equal with that which tears up mountains and carries rocks from one place to another. *The gospel preached is the instrument which God useth for the effecting of it.*

Speaking of the gospel's peacemaking power, he adds,

> It is the chariot wherein the Spirit rides victoriously, when he makes his entrance into the heart of man. . . . He fashions anew the heart, as he framed the world at first, with a word. . . . Power, indeed, to make those who had the seeds of war sown in their very natures against God willing to be friends with him. . . . It strikes many times not only the sinner's sword out of his hand while it is stretched out against God, but the enmity out of his heart, and brings the stoutest rebel upon his knees, humbly to crave the benefit of the articles of peace published in the gospel.[4]

The human heart is the main hindrance preventing our experience of peace with God. It needs the power of God, in and through the gospel (Rom. 1:16), to overcome our hostile hearts. It is thus through his words—in this case, the gospel—that God brings about the most important and most desperately needed peace.

Let the Peace of Christ

The peace that God gives us in Christ, which comes from our reconciled relationship to him, also affects our relationships with others. Peace breeds peace. But Paul takes it a step further in Colossians when he says, "Let the peace of Christ rule in your hearts" (Col. 3:15). The peace that comes from Christ should have control over our hearts, as we navigate difficult matters within

4 William Gurnall, *The Christian in Complete Armour*, vol. 1, direction 7, second general part, https://ccel.org/ (emphasis added).

the body of Christ. Outward peace (with God) produces inner peace, which then enables us to pursue peace in the body. It is noteworthy that in the next verse Paul, still trying to encourage peace in the church, charges them to "let the word of Christ dwell in you richly" (3:16). If the message of Christ has a pervasive presence in congregational life, this will promote peace as well. So Christ and the message of Christ bring spiritual, relational, and inner peace. Elsewhere, Paul speaks of "the peace of God, which surpasses all understanding" that guards our hearts and minds (Phil. 4:7). But he ends that section of the letter calling the believers to put into practice the things that they "have learned and received and heard and seen in me"—that is, Paul's preaching and life—and "the God of peace will be with you" (4:9). Thus in Philippians just as in Colossians, the peace that guards their hearts and minds, alongside the message they received from Paul, produces relational harmony. Peace of all kinds comes through the word of God.

For Those Who Love the Law

The only reference to peace in Psalm 119 is found in this verse. The psalmist writes, "Great peace have those who love your law" (119:165). While the goodness of God comes in the gift of Scripture, the rich experience of that goodness comes chiefly to those who engage Scripture rightly. Here great peace is experienced by those who *love* God's law. What does it look like to love a book, a set of laws, covenant stipulations, promises, and stories of God's faithfulness?

If I love a book, I always find myself coming back to it. This is an especially big deal for a slow reader like me. I come back to a book because in it I have found something that connects me to truth, to reality, to my own heart. The book is transcendent in some way. It is like a wise friend and guide at various seasons in my life. I love certain books because in them I feel seen and understood, or through them I am able to see and understand. Sometimes a book simply just pulls me in and captures my imagination.

The same is true for my son. After he completes a book series—usually a fantasy book series about dragons, talking warrior animals, or wizards—he cannot stop talking about it. He spends almost every spare moment thinking about the story: its high and lows, great scenes, puzzling twists and turns, epic battles. He wants to process the story with anyone who will listen. What my son is doing is meditating on his books. He's chewing on them. He's bringing them into every moment of his day-to-day life.

This is precisely the picture painted in Psalm 1 of the blessed man who meditates on God's law day and night (Ps. 1:2). This image captures the heart of what it is to love the law. In Psalm 119:163, the psalmist says,

> I hate and abhor falsehood,
>   but I love your law.

False ways lead to destruction, but the law leads to life. Perhaps this is why he says,

> Seven times a day I praise you
>   for your righteous rules. (119:164)

Ultimately, why does the psalmist love the law? Because behind the law, he sees a kind and righteous God who desires for him life and not death. Calvin writes,

> From the term *love*, we gather that this peace is not acquired by a slavish observance of the law, but proceeds from faith; for the law has no sweetness to attract us to it, unless it exhibit to us God in the character of a father, and tranquilize our minds by the assurance of eternal salvation.[5]

Those who love God's law experience "great peace" and "nothing can make them stumble." They will enter into *shalom* and avoid the prospect of stumbling, either to destruction and ruin or to distress and a lack of tranquility. In other words, the peace of God, which transcends all understanding, comes to us through God's word—loved and cherished:

> You keep him in perfect peace
> whose mind is stayed on you,
> because he trusts in you. (Isa. 26:3)

---

5 John Calvin, *Commentary on the Book of Psalms*, trans. James Anderson, in *Calvin's Commentaries* (Baker, 2003), 4:41–42.

The peace which God alone reveals,
And by His Word of grace imparts,
Which only the believer feels,
Direct, and keep, and cheer our hearts.

And may the holy Three in One,
The Father, Word, and Comforter,
Pour an abundant blessing down,
On ev'ry soul assembled here.

JOHN NEWTON
"The Peace Which God Alone Reveals"
1792

10

The Gift of Understanding

I have more understanding than all my teachers,
for your testimonies are my meditation.
I understand more than the aged,
for I keep your precepts. . . .

The unfolding of your words gives light;
it imparts understanding to the simple.

PSALM 119:99–100, 130

I STARTED FOLLOWING CHRIST when I was eighteen years old. At that time, I began attending a large Pentecostal church in my hometown. Although the church was a mixed bag socioeconomically, most were not from a middle- or upper-class background. As a new Christian and new attendee, I was immediately embraced by a group of guys who were, at minimum, six years older than I. All of them grew up and were still living in some of the rougher neighborhoods in town. In fact, they were still somewhat rough around the edges. Yet they were kind and generous, and they made an indelible mark on my life in a number of ways during those early days of following Christ.

Among the gifts that these big brothers gave me was a desire to know Scripture with real depth. They regularly had late night and overnight hangouts where they would sit around and discuss issues they were wrestling with in Scripture. For hours they would cross-reference the Bible and debate how to best interpret it. Because I was so new to the Bible, I simply sat in awe of how much they knew Scripture and how much they longed to know it better. If I remember correctly, the majority of them did not have a college degree, and none of them had any formal Bible training. Yet they understood so much. And even though I was college bound and on a different academic trajectory, I wanted to be like them. I wanted to know the Bible. I wanted to be able to speak intelligently about the Christian life. I wanted understanding that outpaced my spiritual maturity and educational background.

In those early days, I encountered a pair of verses in Psalm 119 that captured both my experience and my deepest aspirations. The psalmist writes,

> I have more understanding than all my teachers,
>   for your testimonies are my meditation.
> I understand more than the aged,
>   for I keep your precepts. (Ps. 119:99–100)

This is exactly what I experienced with my big brothers. Even though they did not have formal Bible training, they had real understanding. They were wise beyond their level of education and beyond their years because they regularly meditated on the word of God. Many of our informal conversations and debates were sometimes more enlightening than the Sunday morning fare. They had more understanding than their instructors or elders. Whether they realized it or not, they lived the truth that God's word is where the depths of wisdom and knowledge are found.

The psalmist is not saying that we should aim to learn nothing from teachers or elders, nor is he saying that teachers and elders have nothing to teach us. Rather, he is saying that depth of understanding is not the sole possession of a special class of people. This is strong encouragement for young people and new Christians. Young people can gain real wisdom. In fact, poor people, uneducated people, and all types of non-elites have access to the treasures of God's wisdom and understanding. These are held out to everyone who seeks to take his word seriously and to follow it obediently.

In Psalm 19:7, we read,

> The testimony of the LORD is sure,
> making wise the simple.

Other translations render "the simple" as "the inexperienced." We should never downplay the value of life experience in helping us navigate present and future situations. Those who know things by experience are often our most insightful guides. That's what makes the psalmists' words in both Psalms 19 and 119 so powerful. They speak to those who are perhaps most in danger of folly. And they say that despite not having the life experience of elders, despite not having walked through certain circumstances, and even despite the lack of formal training in biblical studies, we are all still able to find wisdom that surpasses our own personal experiences, or lack thereof. It's almost as if Scripture gives us the knowledge that comes from experience even before we have had those experiences. God's word makes the simple wise.

First Handers vs. Second Handers

Author and pastor John Piper was once asked by a listener of his podcast, "Pastor John, what can I say to my friend that refuses to study the Bible for himself because he thinks he can get all the answers from teachers like you and others online?" This is a really good question that gets to the heart of the psalms we are considering in this chapter. Piper begins his response by reflecting on his days as a student:

> When I was in graduate school in Germany forty-five years ago or so, I was in my twenties. I was surrounded by world-class, high-powered scholarship in people who did not believe the Scriptures as God's word or share my love for the gospel. I knew that, given my limits, I could never read as much as they read or remember as much as they remember or have in my head as many historical facts as they did.[1]

He continues,

> But I took tremendous heart from Psalm 119:99. It had a powerful effect on my perseverance and confidence that God would

1 The following quotes are from John Piper, *Ask Pastor John*, podcast, episode 1533, "Why Do I Need to Read the Bible When We Have Bible Teachers Online?" October 2, 2020, https://www.desiringgod.org/.

> make himself known to me, that he would keep me from doctrinal error, and that he would use me—even as much or more than those folks—to make an impact on the world for his name.

He was especially moved by Psalm 119:99 because of his context: the German university. He studied among those who were at the top of their game in academia. These were *Bible* scholars, those who spent their days poring over the Scriptures in one way or another. Yet Piper saw in the passage a kind of leveling of the playing field. He explains,

> And here's what the verse says: "I have more understanding than all my teachers." Really? How can you say that? Because "your testimonies are my meditation." Now, when the psalmist said that, it's very likely he was talking about esteemed teachers who were looking at the same record of God's word that he was looking at. And the difference is that the psalmist believed that a direct, sustained, personal, love-filled meditation on the word of God itself would produce, in his mind and in his heart, a kind of discernment and a kind of insight that would protect him from errors in his teachers, and indeed, would give him an authentic, personal, true understanding of God and his ways that would go beyond what he got from his teachers, or what they got from their way of study.

Two kinds of people, a scholar and a nonscholar, may diligently study the same Bible, yet the nonscholar may surpass the scholar in understanding. Well-intentioned teachers—even well-intentioned *Bible teachers*—are no substitute for direct engagement with God's word. Piper beautifully concludes his story:

> Now that was enormously important and encouraging and protecting to me. It meant that I didn't feel like I was at the mercy of scholarship. I had access to something so powerful and so precious that by personal, prayerful, sustained, thoughtful, rigorous, love-soaked meditation, I would see things and comprehend things and taste things that these teachers didn't see, didn't comprehend, didn't taste. And frankly, looking back fifty years now, I believe it's true. I believe God granted me to see beautiful things that many of my more sophisticated, even more intelligent, teachers did not see.

He is not discouraging listening to sermons, referring to Bible commentaries, or reading solid Christian books. If he is, how would he make sense of his own ministry? Rather, he is exhorting us to be first-hand readers of the Bible, even while we continue to be aided by Bible teachers and scholars. He asks his listeners the following questions that are also helpful diagnostic questions for all of us:

> Do you believe that having the word of God with you, meditating on it day and night, and obeying it will bear better fruit of insight and wisdom in your life than always depending on other human teachers? That's the question facing you. Do you believe it? Are you content to be a second hander for the rest of your life in view of Psalm 119:99 and what it promises?

If we want deep spiritual understanding, we must commit to be people of one book, even as we continue to be wise consumers of many books.

God's Heart

The hunger for wisdom and understanding is a good thing. The story of Solomon is illuminating and encouraging in this regard. At the beginning of his reign, God appears to Solomon—who at this point is faithful in most things but with some caveats—and invites him to ask anything of him. The king, as is well known, asks God to give him "an understanding mind to govern your people, that I may discern between good and evil, for who is able to govern this your great people?" (1 Kings 3:9). Solomon's request pleased the Lord so much that God responds, "Behold, I give you a wise and discerning mind, so that none like you has been before you and none like you shall arise after you" (3:12), and he gives him incomparable wealth and honor as well.

Three things are clear from this story. The first is that God is the source of understanding, as the one who, in himself, has infinite understanding:

> Behold, God is mighty, and does not despise any;
> he is mighty in strength of understanding. (Job 36:5)

> The Lord by wisdom founded the earth;
> by understanding he established the heavens. (Prov. 3:19)

He who has gives. Second, as we just saw, God delights in our desire for understanding, especially when he is seen as the source and others are viewed as beneficiaries. The last thing we see is that God takes pleasure in granting understanding not sparingly but in abundance. Solomon did not receive scraps from the table of

God's understanding but became world renowned for his wisdom and discernment.

Words + Power = Understanding

All that we've reflected on points to the simple math behind the acquisition of understanding. Scripture gives us the equation. It begins in Deuteronomy 4:6, where Moses, speaking of the Lord's commands, says to Israel, "Keep them and do them, for that will be your wisdom and your understanding in the sight of the peoples, who, when they hear all these statutes, will say, 'Surely this great nation is a wise and understanding people.'" What defines Israel as an understanding people is the presence of God's word among them and, more so, their obedience to it.

The second part of the equation is drawn from the apostle Paul when he encourages the Colossian church, "We have not ceased to pray for you, asking that you may be filled with the knowledge of his will in all spiritual wisdom and understanding" (Col. 1:9). Those who have already received the gospel and are bearing fruit are still dependent on God for spiritual understanding.

So this is the equation: God's word plus God's gracious power yields spiritual understanding. In fact, Paul says elsewhere, "Think over what I say [that is, my words of exhortation], for the Lord will give you understanding in everything" (2 Tim. 2:7). Our openness and obedience to God's word is the context in which he works powerfully to give us more understanding than our enemies, our teachers, and even our elders.

—

To Thee, the Author of the Book,
O Lord, in humble faith we look;
Explain to us the sacred page,
And let its truth our hearts engage.

Instruct the teacher and the taught;
Unfold the page with wisdom fraught;
Open to us the hidden store
Which makes us rich for evermore.

AUTHOR UNKNOWN
"To Thee, the Author of the Book"
1911

11

The Gift of Sight

Make me understand the way of your precepts,
and I will meditate on your wondrous works.

PSALM 119:27

WHEN I WAS A CHILD, my favorite after-school ritual was watching a cartoon called *ThunderCats*. One of the things I loved most about this show was the weapon known as the "sword of omens," which was wielded by the main character, Lion-O. The sword had a number of amazing features, but perhaps one was the greatest of all: Whenever Lion-O would lift the hilt of the sword to eye level and say, "Sword of omens, give me sight beyond sight!" the hilt would then become like a set of binoculars that enabled him to see hidden enemies, view distant places, and even find imperiled team members. "Sight beyond sight" was a game changer. It regularly turned hopeless situations around by providing Lion-O with insights that helped him know what to do next. When he was lost and in despair, he needed "sight beyond sight." He needed the ability to see beyond his current situation.

I have terrible eyesight. When I get up in the middle of the night and forget (or choose not) to put on my eyeglasses, it can be a dangerous affair. I may bump my knee against the bench at the end of our bed. I am likely to hit the corner of the dresser as I turn into our bathroom. By the time I get back into bed, I might get battered and bruised—all for a short trip to the bathroom. Mornings are a little better. But if you asked me to tell you the time on our alarm clock or the expression on my wife's face, I simply wouldn't be able to tell you. I can make out the general outline of things, but the details are lost to me.

We often have blurry vision when it comes to our lives. This may be the result of our history, our family, our present hardships, or something as benign as immaturity. Whatever the reason, we sometimes find ourselves incapable of seeing what God is doing in our lives with any clarity. So we end up battered and bruised or simply incapable of enjoying the gifts of God.

We need clarity. We need glasses. We need sight beyond sight. This is why God gives us the gift of Scripture.

First Sight

We rightly speak of Scripture as God's revelation. Well, what does God's revelation reveal? In short, God and his works. God's word—the Law, the Prophets, the Gospels, and more—has the same agenda and scope: to reveal the mighty works of God to the praise of God. Our psalmist's prayer in this passage aligns with what Scripture is all about. He prays,

> Make me understand the way of your precepts,
> and [or "so that"] I will meditate on your wondrous works. (Ps. 119:27)

There are two things to observe here. First, the psalmist acknowledges that depth of understanding of God's word—not just of the sentences and phrases but also its goodness and significance—must come from God himself. Spurgeon writes of this prayer,

> It is a confession of a good man who may understand a great deal, but feels that he does not understand all. In this learning, he who understands most is the man who thinks he understands least. He who has the clearest knowledge of Divine things is the very one to feel that there is a boundless ocean far beyond his observation.[1]

The psalmist asks God to help him know, with greater depth, what the precepts mean and, more importantly, how he is to apply them. God's word is a many-splendored wonder. He wants to see its beauty and riches from every angle. The psalmist simply reminds us that when we think of God's word, we cannot separate the author from the illuminator. The same Spirit who breathed out these Scriptures gives its recipients deep and insider understanding of its meaning and significance—that is, what it's saying and why it matters.

Yet the purpose of this longed-for understanding is that he will meditate on God's "wondrous works." The wonders refer to

1 Charles H. Spurgeon, "The Student's Prayer," Sermon 1344, *Spurgeon's Sermons*, vol. 23, https://ccel.org/.

the works of God revealed in the law: the works of creation and redemption. To paraphrase the passage, "Lord, help me understand your law, so that I can meditate more deeply on your works revealed in it." This is what we might call the desire for "first sight": to see God's mighty deeds rightly as the psalmist sees God's word in a fresh light. He yearns to know and feel the wonder of the things that God has done in the past for his people, and this comes only as he understands more deeply God's word.

Second Sight

But if we view the psalmist as writing from within the context of trial and hardship, then perhaps this passage has a richer meaning. We have to ask what is the value of meditating on God's wondrous works for someone in the midst of tribulation. I think the psalmist is implying that whatever his situation, he needs to interpret it in light of God's wonders revealed in Scripture. As he meditates on God's goodness and faithfulness in the past, he is able to reassess where he stands in the present. For him, the events of the exodus loom large; for us, it is the work of Christ and the gift of his Spirit. The bleakness of the psalmist's circumstances must be viewed anew through the lens of God's mighty works.

Recalling God's mighty works to reframe one's view of the present is a common theme in Scripture. On the "day of trouble," the psalmist regularly offers the encouragement to "remember the deeds of the Lord" (Ps. 77:2, 11). This is captured vividly in one episode of Israel's history. As Israel was on the verge of entering the promised land, Moses gives an inspiring speech about how God wants to bless them, keep them from sickness, and make them fruitful in every way. He then reminds them of God's promise:

"And you shall consume all the peoples that the Lord your God will give over to you" (Deut. 7:16). Yet he anticipates that fear may creep into their hearts when they stand face-to-face with the nations they are meant to dispossess. Hear his counsel:

> If you say in your heart, "These nations are greater than I. How can I dispossess them?" you shall not be afraid of them but you shall remember what the Lord your God did to Pharaoh and to all Egypt, the great trials that your eyes saw, the signs, the wonders, the mighty hand, and the outstretched arm, by which the Lord your God brought you out. So will the Lord your God do to all the peoples of whom you are afraid. (Deut. 7:17–19)

When fear grips their hearts, he tells them to *remember*. This act of recollection helps them reinterpret their situation. Rather than telling themselves a false story of inevitable defeat, death, and humiliation before their enemies, recalling God's prior redemptive acts will enable them to believe a true story—the story of God fulfilling his promise to give them the land pledged to Abraham, Isaac, and Jacob.

Scripture, thus, gives us what I'm calling "second sight": It opens our eyes to God's wondrous works in history ("first sight"), which then helps us see our current circumstances with greater clarity, reinterpreting our lives in light of God's real and active presence ("second sight").

Reading Glasses

The lens metaphor is a significant one in the history of Christian thought. Calvin makes use of the image to explain the role of

Scripture in helping us make sense of God's revelation in creation. He speaks of how creation makes God's presence known to all people "without exception." Yet a "better help" is needed to lead us to worship God as the Creator of the cosmos. This better help is the "light of his Word" by which God becomes "known unto salvation." Then comes the beautiful metaphor:

> Just as old or bleary-eyed men and those with weak vision, if you thrust before them a most beautiful volume, even if they recognize it to be some sort of writing, yet can scarcely construe two words, but with the aid of spectacles will begin to read distinctly; so Scripture, gathering up the otherwise confused knowledge of God in our minds, having dispersed our dullness, clearly shows us the true God.[2]

God really does speak through creation, and he is an articulate communicator. But our sin and ignorance make us bleary-eyed so that our knowledge of God can be "confused." The Scriptures are the spectacles, the lenses, through which we are enabled to see God and all his works with clarity and in such a way that benefits our souls. Calvin concludes, "Therefore, however fitting it may be for man seriously to turn his eyes to contemplate God's works, since he has been placed in this most glorious theater to be a spectator of them, it is fitting that he prick up his ears to the Word, the better to profit."[3] What a wonderful image! We've been placed in a "glorious theater" to be spectators of God's creative

2 John Calvin, *Institutes of the Christian Religion*, ed. John T. McNeill, trans. Ford Lewis Battles, 2 vols., Library of Christian Classics 20–21 (Westminster John Knox, 2006), 1.6.1.

3 Calvin, *Institutes*, 1.6.2.

and providential activity. Yet just as it is easy to look at a difficult situation and come to the wrong conclusion about what God is doing, we can look at creation and come to poor conclusions about God (see Rom. 1:18–23). So if we want to know and experience the goodness of what God is doing in our lives and in all creation, we must view them through our biblical eyeglasses.

Through Scripture we are better able to see our place in the unfolding drama of creation, redemption, and new creation. Scripture gives us the gift of sight beyond sight.

—

'Tis by the faith of joys to come
We walk thro' deserts dark as night;
Till we arrive at heav'n, our home,
Truth is our guide, and faith our light.

The want of sight she well supplies;
She makes the pearly gates appear;
Far into distant worlds she pries,
And brings eternal glories near.

ISAAC WATTS
"'Tis by Faith of Joys to Come"
1776

12

The Gift of Nourishment

I open my mouth and pant,
because I long for your commandments.

PSALM 119:131

THE WORD OF GOD is food for our souls. We regularly sing songs that emphasize our dependence on God for sustenance. God himself says to Israel,

> I am the LORD your God,
> who brought you up out of the land of Egypt.
> Open your mouth wide, and I will fill it. (Ps. 81:10)

Yet just as we are meant to be satisfied with God's steadfast love (Ps. 90:14), his word is meant to nourish us and fill our souls to overflowing. Put another way, one of the main ways God satisfies our famished souls is by giving us his words to feed on. The psalmist in our passage prays,

I open my mouth and pant,
because I long for your commandments. (Ps 119:131)

Like a hungry and thirsty traveler desperate for any kind of sustenance, the psalmist comes to God's word, looking to be fed. Daniel Estes notes, "The psalmist depicts himself as a young bird with its mouth open to receive food. This image implies that he is eating necessary nutrition, not an optional snack or dessert. Far from accepting God's word out of a sense of obligation, he pants and longs for God's commands."[1] When God speaks, he is able to satisfy the deepest needs of the soul.

Bread of Heaven

Jesus had just miraculously fed more than five thousand people off the coast of the Sea of Galilee. The crowds are astonished, and hope begins to mount that he is indeed the longed-for Messiah, the "Prophet who is to come into the world" (John 6:14). Sensing that they were going to try to make him king, he withdraws for a while. A little later in the day, his disciples set sail to return to their homebase of Capernaum without Jesus. Then comes the storm. And then comes Jesus calming the storm. The next day, the crowd that had been fed realizes that Jesus and his disciples are no longer there. So they get into boats and head for Capernaum, looking for Jesus.

The story gathers steam when they finally find him. They ask him, "Rabbi, when did you come here?" (6:25). Rather than answering their fairly straightforward question, Jesus cuts the

1 Daniel J. Estes, *Psalms 73–150*, in The New American Commentary (B&H, 2019), 430.

small talk and goes to the heart of the matter: "Truly, truly, I say to you, you are seeking me, not because you saw signs, but because you ate your fill of the loaves" (6:26). This is a strange accusation. Elsewhere in the Gospels, Jesus indicts his opponents or chastises the crowds because all they want are signs. Here, signs and wonders are not the big draw—a full belly is. Jesus cautions them, "Do not work for the food that perishes, but for the food that endures to eternal life, which the Son of Man will give to you" (6:27). Jesus explains that the work required to get the food that he provides is to believe in him. It is only at this point that they demand a sign, completely missing what he just said: "Our fathers ate the manna in the wilderness" (6:31). In other words, "Prove yourself, Jesus! Give us another food miracle like Moses did!" They're demanding this even though he had just miraculously fed them on the other side of the Sea of Galilee, something to which they can testify.

"Truly, truly," Jesus responds, "it was not Moses who gave you bread from heaven, but my Father gives you the true bread from heaven. For the bread of God is he who comes down from heaven and gives life to the world" (6:32–33). And then comes the key line: "I am the bread of life; whoever comes to me shall not hunger, and whoever believes in me shall never thirst" (6:35). The feeding of the five thousand is one big setup. Its narrative purpose is to highlight a singular point: Jesus is the ultimate soul food. We must eat his flesh and drink his blood, if we want to have eternal life (6:53–57). His flesh is "true food" and his blood "true drink" (6:55). What is Jesus getting at?

Throughout church history, these verses have been used to defend various interpretations of the Lord's Supper, but we can ignore those debates here. What is clear is that eating and drinking Jesus has to do with what he said earlier about working for "the food that endures to eternal life" (6:27). That work, as we saw, is to believe in Jesus. This is repeated later when he says that the way to partake of the bread of life is to believe in him (6:35). Eating is believing. Yet believing in Jesus is inseparable from believing the words that he speaks. This is why the crowds ask for a sign so that they might believe him—that is, in what he is saying (6:30). This is also why this episode culminates with Peter's beautiful confession: "Lord, to whom shall we go? You have *the words* of eternal life" (6:68). Peter and the disciples feasted on Jesus as the true bread from heaven. But they also recognized that to feed on this bread required that they feed on his words. The food of the word gives access to a feast of life-giving flesh and blood.

Not Only Bread

Jesus's interaction with the crowds in this Gospel episode recalls the most important miraculous feeding in Israel's history, at least prior to his miraculous feedings of thousands—the provision of manna in the wilderness. The story is familiar. The people of Israel are wandering in the desert, just shortly after the defeat of Pharaoh and his army at the Red Sea. They are really hungry, so they start complaining about their food options, especially in comparison to what they ate as slaves in Egypt (Ex. 16:1–3). God then provides them with "bread from heaven," along with stipulations on when and how much to gather to "test them, whether they will walk in my law" (16:4).

When Israel is on the cusp of entering the promised land, Moses recalls this episode and provides a pastoral interpretation of what God was really doing in his provision of manna. He says to the people,

> And you shall remember the whole way that the LORD your God has led you these forty years in the wilderness, that he might humble you, testing you to know what was in your heart, whether you would keep his commandments or not. And he humbled you and let you hunger and fed you with manna, which you did not know, nor did your fathers know, that he might make you know that man does not live by bread alone, but man lives by every word that comes from the mouth of the LORD. (Deut. 8:2–3)

God let his redeemed people starve so that he could miraculously feed them. Yet the miraculous feeding—and the awe that it might elicit—was not the only goal. The Lord wanted to test and teach his people. He wanted to *test* whether they would wholeheartedly trust and obey his words. He wanted to *teach* them that life as God's people in God's world is not a matter of food and drink, or even of receiving miraculous bread from heaven.

Charles Spurgeon, in a sermon on this passage, marvels at something we often miss as we seek to apply these verses.[2] He remarks on how it is a wonder that bread should have the power to sustain the human body: "The process is a very wonderful one by which bread turns into flesh, and blood, and bone, and muscle,

2 The following quotes are from Charles H. Spurgeon, "Living on the Word," March 15, 1883, in *Metropolitan Tabernacle Pulpit*, vol. 44, https://www.spurgeon.org/.

and hair, and all sorts of things, by a perpetual working of the power of God." But even more marvelous is how physical food keeps both body and spirit alive. He admits, "And how is it that the material substance in bread somehow works to the keeping of our spirit in connection with this flesh and blood? I cannot explain this mystery, but I believe it to be a continual miracle wrought by God." The point for Spurgeon is that, in a superior yet equally mysterious and marvelous way, God uses his word to sustain body and soul.

The *word* in our passage likely refers to God's law and promises. God's laws are to be obeyed; his promises are to be trusted. In these ways, Israel remains a faithful covenant partner and recipient of God's blessings. Spurgeon helpfully makes much of "every word," observing that we all have favorite aspects of Scripture that we tend to privilege to the neglect of others, whether they be doctrines, precepts, promises, histories, prophecies, and threats or warnings. His counsel?

> If you restrict yourselves in your food to one or two articles, every physician will tell you that there is a danger that your body may not be supplied with every form of nutriment that it requires. A good wide range of diet is recommended to those who would have vigorous health. And in spiritual things, if you keep to one part of God's Word, you may live on it, but the tendency will be for you not to attain to complete spiritual health through the lack of some nutriment with which the Word would have supplied you had you used it all. Every Word of God is that upon which man lives in the highest and healthiest state.

No matter how the word comes to us—a voice from heaven, in a cloud, on a mountain, in tablets of stone, on parchment, in the Son, or in a book—Spurgeon encourages us, "Let it be to you, spiritually, your house, your home, your food, your medicine, your clothing, the one essential element of your soul's life and growth." He says to us, as he did to his congregation almost a hundred and fifty years ago, "Oh, keep to the Word, my brothers! Keep to it as God's Word, and as coming out of his mouth. Suck it down into your soul; you cannot have too much of it. Feed on it day and night, for thus will God make you to live the life that is life indeed."

Only the word can sustain hope, joy, and connection to the life of God, especially when bread ceases to fall from the sky.

Thou art the Bread of Life,
O Lord, to me,
Thy holy Word the truth
That saveth me;
Give me to eat and live
With Thee above;
Teach me to love Thy truth,
For Thou art Love.

MARY A. LATHBURY
"Break Thou the Bread of Life"
1877

There is a Storehouse of rich fare,
Supplied with plenty and to spare;
'Tis God's own Word! It spreads a feast
For every hungering, thirsty guest.

H. J. BETTS
"Thy Word a Lamp"
1911

13

The Gift of Strength in Affliction

If your law had not been my delight,
I would have perished in my affliction.
PSALM 119:92

AT THE BEGINNING of *The Problem of Pain*, C. S. Lewis recalls that in his days as an atheist, if anyone asked him why he did not believe in God, he would have pointed to the existence of pain, suffering, and death in the world God supposedly created. "If you ask me to believe that this is the work of a benevolent and omnipotent spirit," he writes, "I reply that all the evidence points in the opposite direction. Either there is no spirit behind the universe, or else a spirit indifferent to good and evil, or else an evil spirit."[1] Brutal honesty from Lewis, the former atheist. But one does not need to be an atheist to acknowledge the relentless presence of suffering in the world. The existence of lament psalms

1 C. S. Lewis, *The Problem of Pain* (HarperOne, 1996), 3.

testifies to the reality of suffering, even for God's people. In fact, the humiliation of the Son of God places suffering at the very heart of creation's story.

Suffering is woven into the fabric of human life. It is never a question of *if* we will suffer. It's a matter of when, how, how severe, and for how long. The Puritan Samuel Rutherford captures this truth in a letter written in 1637:

> For I am persuaded, it is a piece of the chief errand of our life, that God sent us for some years down to this earth, among devils and men, the fire-brands of the devil, and temptations, that we might suffer for a time here amongst our enemies; otherwise he might have made heaven to wait on us, at our coming out of the womb, and have carried us home to our country, without letting us set down our feet in this knotty and thorny life.

He then concludes,

> But seeing a piece of suffering is carved to every one of us, less or more, as Infinite Wisdom hath thought good, our part is to harden and habituate our soft and thin-skinned nature to endure fire and water, devils, lions, men, losses, [sorrowful] hearts as those that are looked upon by God, angels, men and devils.[2]

Once we've accepted suffering to be a fact of life, ordained in some mysterious way by our wise God himself, the question then becomes, "How do we bear up under it?"

2 Rutherford to Earlston Younger, 1637 in *Letters of Samuel Rutherford* (Banner of Truth, 2012), 97–98.

A Matter of Perspective?

At least part of the answer is that we must adopt the right perspective on our suffering. A wrong perspective only exacerbates our pain. Tim Keller highlights five different cultural perspectives on suffering, each naming a different cause and calling for a different response. The first perspective is the *moralistic*, which sees suffering as caused by the failure of people to live rightly. Karma is an example of this approach. The second perspective he calls the *self-transcendent* view, which holds that suffering derives from unfulfilled desires. Suffering is alleviated by detaching from transient things of this world or from a sense of individuality—both of which give a false picture of reality and therefore cause us pain. Third, certain cultures hold a view of suffering as *fate*, a destiny chosen for us out of the inscrutable will of God. The way to bear up under it is simply to accept it without question. According to the fourth perspective, *dualism*, we suffer as pawns in a battle between the cosmic powers of good and evil. The final view is *secularism*, which holds that suffering is an accidental and meaningless interruption in our lives. The only way to deal with it is to manage the pain or eliminate the cause of pain through techniques like therapy or even medication.[3]

Most of these approaches rightly acknowledge suffering, and most of them try to make sense of it. Yet they all differ from the biblical picture, and the difference is significant. Keller summarizes this difference:

> Christianity teaches that, contra fatalism, suffering is overwhelming; contra Buddhism, suffering is real; contra karma,

3 Timothy Keller, *Walking with God Through Pain and Suffering* (Dutton, 2013), 17–31.

> suffering is often unfair; but contra secularism, suffering is meaningful. There is purpose to it, it can drive us like a nail deep into the love of God and into more stability and spiritual power than you can imagine.[4]

Suffering can drive us more deeply into God. So there's purpose in it but also a presence within and through it.

The One Who Sees

One of the most powerful names of God in Scripture is given by an Egyptian concubine. After being cast out with her child by Abram and Sarah, Hagar encounters the angel of the Lord, who says to her, "The Lord has listened to your affliction" (Gen. 16:11). We are not told if Hagar has even prayed (though she may have). We are told that God took it on himself to care for Hagar as he saw her affliction. He promises a wonderful future for her and her son. As a result, she "names" God, calling him "You are a God who sees me" (16:13 ESV mg.), and the well close by is named Beer-lahai-roi, meaning "well of the living One who sees me" (16:14 ESV mg.).

Later on in Scripture's story, when Moses encounters God at the burning bush, he is told by the Lord, "I have surely seen the affliction of my people who are in Egypt and have heard their cry because of their taskmasters. I know their sufferings, and I have come down to deliver them" (Ex. 3:7–8). God sees our affliction; he knows our suffering. He comes down to aid us. In fact, the apostle Paul speaks of the Father as the "God of all comfort, who

4 Keller, *Walking with God*, 30.

comforts us in all our affliction" (2 Cor. 1:3–4). God is with us in our hardships. In fact, in Christ, God has entered into our world of suffering, taken on pain, and infused suffering with all the meaning in the world by working redemption through it. All who suffer abundantly in Christ will receive abundant comfort through Christ (1:5). God's presence in suffering is the most important thing we need to know as we try to put suffering in context.

One of the most difficult aspects of suffering is how isolating it feels. While we know that we are not the only ones to have ever suffered, it often feels like no one else understands our pain.

> The heart knows its own bitterness,
>   and no stranger shares its joy. (Prov. 14:10)

We often feel like we must suffer in silence alone. But if we follow Paul's train of thought, we can see God's better design. God "comforts us in all our affliction," he writes, "so that we may be able to comfort those who are in any affliction, with the comfort with which we ourselves are comforted by God" (2 Cor. 1:4). Other recipients of comfort are meant to comfort us in our afflictions, and vice versa. Not only does God provide his presence, but he also provides the presence of others.

A Faithful Companion

By God's design, we are meant to have at least two companions with us in our sufferings: God and comforted sufferers. But our passage includes a third. The psalmist writes,

> If your law had not been my delight,
> I would have perished in my affliction. (Ps. 119:92)

God's law is a companion whose delightful company enabled the psalmist to bear up under his sufferings. In an earlier stanza, the psalmist writes,

> Let your mercy come to me, that I may live;
> for your law is my delight. (119:77)

His basis for appealing to God's mercy is that he delights in God's law. While God doesn't always act as we would like in response to our obedience, the psalmist knows he can have greater confidence in the Lord because God is faithful to those who are faithful to his covenant law. In 119:92, therefore, the psalmist may simply be saying that God delivered him from affliction because he delights in the law.

The law, however, may have also helped in a number of other ways. For instance, it may have been a source of consolation to the psalmist. Calvin writes,

> He confirms from his own experience . . . that there is no other solace, and no other remedy for adversity, but our reposing upon the word of God, and our embracing the grace and assurance of our salvation which are offered in it. . . . The prophet declares that he was grievously oppressed by a weight of afflictions enough to overwhelm him; but that the consolation which he derived from the Divine Law in such desperate circumstances, was as life to him.[5]

5 John Calvin, *Commentary on the Book of Psalms*, trans. James Anderson, in *Calvin's Commentaries* (Baker, 2003), 4:471.

Or God's word may have helped him find meaning in his affliction, taught him how to respond to adversity, instructed him to seek forgiveness, and encouraged him to refrain from certain behaviors in the midst of trial.[6] In these varied ways, the psalmist was not left alone to fend for himself.

The near and comforting presence of God's law is all the more marvelous if we consider how this stanza begins. We read,

> Forever, O Lord, your word
> is firmly fixed in the heavens. (119:89)

The first line can also be translated "Your word is eternal," "Your word is forever," or "Your word endures forever." The kinds of attributes we would normally ascribe to God are here attached to his word. This is the strongest of affirmations of the fixedness and eternality of God's self-communication, which takes concrete form in his law and commandments. As the stanza unfolds, it becomes clear that this eternal and heavenly word is the very word God has given to sustain the psalmist in the midst of trial. The transcendent becomes immanent, to put it in theological speak. God's world-sustaining and covenant-making word is gifted to us as a companion, preparing us for and sustaining us in our suffering.

---

6 See Willem A. VanGemeren, *Psalms*, in *The Expositor's Bible Commentary*, vol. 5 (Zondervan, 2007), 752; Daniel J. Estes, *Psalms 73–150*, in The New American Commentary (B&H, 2019), 422; Tremper Longman III, *Psalms: An Introduction and Commentary*, in Tyndale Old Testament Commentaries 15–16 (IVP Academic, 2014), 406.

How firm a foundation, ye saints of the Lord,
Is laid for your faith in His excellent word!
What more can He say than to you He hath said,
To you who for refuge to Jesus have fled?

ATTRIBUTED TO ROBERT KEEN
"How Firm a Foundation"
1787

14

The Gift of True Truth

Your righteousness is righteous forever,
and your law is true. . . .

But you are near, O Lord,
and all your commandments are true. . . .

The sum of your word is truth,
and every one of your righteous
rules endures forever.

PSALM 119:142, 151, 160

The rules of the Lord *are true,*
and righteous altogether.

PSALM 19:9

WHEN I WAS A CHILD, one word I said more often than my mother would have liked was "Why?" No matter the topic, I wanted to know why that was the case. "Why did we go this way and not that?" "Why are you asking me to do this and not that?" "Why does this rule exist?" I could not stand easy answers or answers that didn't make sense to my five-, eight-, or twelve-year-old brain. My mom would often say, in a somewhat exasperated tone, "Son, you should be a lawyer!" As annoying as I was, what I was really searching for was something solid, something I could trust that could guide my actions. In my own childish way, I was searching for truth and not just an opinion.

Several years ago, Francis Beckwith and Gregory Koukl published a popular primer on moral relativism called *Relativism: Feet Firmly Planted in Mid-Air*.[1] That subtitle and the image it evokes have stuck with me over the years as I've thought about the issue of truth. Feet cannot be "firmly planted" in mid-air because there is nothing firm on which to stand. We are like astronauts floating around in zero gravity, untethered and unrooted. Trying to stand up and walk is an impossibility. Truth is an anchor and a center; it is a core and foundation. Without it, there is no knowledge and no morality. To put it less philosophically, without truth, there is nothing *for* which and *from* which to live.

What Is Truth?

During his trial before Pilate, Jesus says that his mission was "to bear witness to the truth" (John 18:37). He adds that everyone "who is of the truth" listens to his voice. In response, Pilate asks the all-important question: "What is truth?" (18:38).

In the previous chapter of John's gospel, Jesus gives an answer to this question. When he was praying for his disciples shortly

1 Francis Beckwith and Gregory Koukl, *Relativism: Feet Firmly Planted in Mid-Air* (Baker, 1998).

before his arrest, he asks the Father to "sanctify them in the truth" (17:17). And when he goes on to clarify what the "truth" is, he says, "Your word is truth." What comes out of God's mouth, and what is declared by Jesus, the apostles, the prophets, psalms, and torah is truth. This is a profound statement, especially given that just a bit earlier, Jesus declares himself "the way, *the truth*, and the life" (14:6), and speaks of the Spirit as "the Spirit of truth" (14:17; 15:26; 16:13). Whatever truth is, it is at the core of who God is as Father, Son, and Spirit, and it captures all that the triune God has to say to us for the purpose of giving us life and a kingdom.

In Scripture, *truth* is used in three broad senses. The first is what we might call an intellectual sense, referring to whether something is factually correct, corresponding to reality, or faithful to a standard (e.g., Deut. 17:4). The second sense refers to truth as a personal or moral category. To be of the truth, in this sense, means that someone or something has a dependable, reliable, faithful, or consistent character (e.g., Gen. 42:16). In fact, one Hebrew word for *truth* is sometimes translated "faithfulness" (e.g., Ex. 34:6). The third sense refers to what is complete and real, as opposed to what is lacking and false (e.g., Mark 5:33). All three ways of speaking about truth are related and cannot be easily separated. For example, a truthful person aims to speak what is factually true and live in a way that corresponds to reality. The Bible often speaks of God as true or truthful, meaning that he is faithful, trustworthy, and consistent. He is true—that is, faithful—in his loving care for his people and in his opposition toward sin (Gen. 32:9–12; Ps. 54:5). Truth also extends to God's actions. He judges in truth (Ps. 96:13) and sends out his truth (57:3). In the end, truth is what is real, complete, faithful, and trustworthy.[2] It is ultimately a person—Father, Son, and Spirit—but it also refers to what comes from God.

The Sum Total of the Word

Given that truth describes God and what he does, it should not be surprising that his word is described in similar ways. In one of our passages, two attributes characterize God's word: truthfulness and faithfulness:

> The sum of your word is truth,
> and every one of your righteous rules endures forever.
> (Ps. 119:160)

One commentator translates it as, "Truthfulness is the sum total of your word, every faithful decision of yours stands forever."[3] God's word is an expression and extension of himself. Just as he is truthful and faithful, so his word is truthful and faithful. Or as another commentator puts it, "Each of the Lord's righteous standards is everlasting, not failing and never expiring. There is no hint of falseness or chance of failure in anything God has said. God's people can trust what he says because they trust the God who has said it."[4] God's word is reliable, trustworthy, and

2 See F. H. Palmer, "Truth," in *New Bible Dictionary* (InterVarsity Press, 1996), 1225; D. K. Clark, "Truth," in *Evangelical Dictionary of Theology*, 3rd ed., ed. Daniel J. Treier and Walter A. Elwell (Baker Academic, 2017), 901.

3 John Goldingay, *Psalms*, 3 vols., Baker Commentary on the Old Testament (Baker, 2006), 3:438.

4 Daniel J. Estes, *Psalms 73–150*, in The New American Commentary (B&H, 2019), 436.

complete, lacking in nothing. It is able to give us all we need to build a life before him.

This full-orbed notion of Scripture as truth is much of what the post-Reformation tradition tried to capture in its teaching on the sufficiency of Scripture. The Belgic Confession, an early Reformed statement of faith, emphatically states, "We believe that this Holy Scripture contains the will of God completely and that everything one must believe to be saved is sufficiently taught in it." Then it goes on to weave together many of the truth themes we've encountered, such as truth as a foundation, as complete, as contrary to falsehood, as the absolute standard. It reads,

> For since the entire manner of service which God requires of us is described in it at great length, no one—even an apostle or an angel from heaven, as Paul says—ought to teach other than what the Holy Scriptures have already taught us.
>
> For since it is forbidden to add to the Word of God, or take anything away from it, it is plainly demonstrated that the teaching is perfect and complete in all respects.
>
> Therefore we must not consider human writings—no matter how holy their authors may have been—equal to the divine writings; nor may we put custom, nor the majority, nor age, nor the passage of times or persons, nor councils, decrees, or official decisions above the truth of God, for truth is above everything else.
>
> For all human beings are liars by nature and more vain than vanity itself.
>
> Therefore we reject with all our hearts everything that does not agree with this infallible rule, as we are taught to do by

> the apostles when they say, "Test the spirits to see whether they are from God," and also, "Do not receive into the house or welcome anyone who comes to you and does not bring this teaching."[5]

Just like the elementary-age version of me needed solid truth to guide my actions, so we need God's truthfulness, reflected in Scripture, to lead us into a faithful life before the Lord. And because all other truths are partial, lacking, and merely human, God graciously gave us something sure that we can constantly come back to when all around us seems unclear or proves untrustworthy. In a creaturely way that reflects God himself, Scripture is "perfect and complete in all respects." This truth stands above everything else and is the "infallible rule" and rock on which we stand.

True Truth

Even as Christians, we are always in danger of allowing something to usurp the place of God's truth in our lives. Whether it be our own rationality, feelings, or cultural perspectives on what could possibly be good, right, or true, we can sometimes orient ourselves around something less than God's truth. The twentieth century apologist and writer Francis Schaeffer saw this relativizing of truth as among the greatest challenges facing the church. He lamented a lapsing confidence in the truths of God's revelation among Christians and argued that if the church was to bear witness to Christ and step into the brokenness of the world, it must hold tenaciously to what he called "true truth." He explains,

5 "Belgic Confession," in *Creeds, Confessions, and Catechisms: A Reader's Edition*, ed. Chad B. Van Dixhoorn (Crossway, 2022), 82–83 (art. 7).

> The biblical presentation is that, though we do not have exhaustive truth, we have from the Bible what I term "true truth." In this way we know true truth about God, true truth about man and something truly about nature. Thus on the basis of the Scriptures, while we do not have exhaustive knowledge, we have true and unified knowledge.[6]

By "true truth," Schaeffer is referring to absolute truth, something that he believes was being relinquished in the church, university, and society. Yet for him, true truth was not merely a set of propositions to be believed, though it was that primarily; it was also something to be lived. He writes, "Historic Christianity, biblical Christianity, believes that Christianity is not just doctrinal truth, but flaming truth—true to what is there, true to the great final environment, the infinite-personal God."[7] It is from this center of personal-doctrinal truth that Christians go out, not solely to declare the good news but also to make sense of the world for the sake of the world. From the standpoint of true truth, we can understand and appreciate lesser truths. We can interpret the times and discern between the beauty and chaos of culture. It is only with a commitment to true truth that we can point the world to the God of truth, the only true God, the very source and end of all that we deem to be true, beautiful, good, and worthy of our energies.

C. S. Lewis said that Christianity has the remarkable and unique capacity to fit science, art, morality, and even non-Christian religions within its worldview. This led him to conclude famously,

6 Francis A. Schaeffer, *Escape from Reason* (InterVarsity Press, 2014), 29.

7 Francis A. Schaeffer, *The Great Evangelical Disaster* (Crossway, 1995), 81.

"I believe in Christianity as I believe that the Sun has risen not only because I see it but because by it I see everything else."[8] Scripture is the gift of God's truth, a truth in which we can truly rest and a truth from which we build, by God's grace, a God-pleasing and world-shaping life.

Hail, sacred Truth! whose piercing rays
Dispel the shades of night;
Diffusing o'er the mental world
The healing beams of light.

Thy Word, O Lord, with friendly aid,
Restores our wand'ring feet,
Converts the sorrows of the mind
To joys divinely sweet.

O send Thy light and truth abroad
In all their radiant blaze,
And bid th'admiring world adore
The glories of Thy grace.

JOHN BUTTRESS
"Hail, Sacred Truth"
1817

8 C. S. Lewis, "Is Theology Poetry? A Paper," in *Screwtape Proposes a Toast and Other Pieces* (Fontana, 1965), 58.

15

The Gift of Freedom

I will walk freely in an open place
because I study your precepts.

PSALM 119:45 CSB

"WE HOLD THESE TRUTHS to be self-evident, that all men are created equal, that they are endowed by their Creator with certain unalienable Rights, that among these are Life, Liberty and the pursuit of Happiness." We have a right—a right granted by God, inherent to what we are as humans—to be free, so says the Declaration of Independence. I grew up in Canada, yet I've always admired the American commitment to liberty, which is something not particularly characteristic of the Canadian mindset. While we value liberty (and who wouldn't?), it isn't the life breath of Canadian social and political culture. The United States was founded on the principle of liberty, national and individual; Canada was not. Far from being merely an Americanism, freedom is a concern for God himself. But because the language of freedom is so much a part of

American life, it requires more care when dealing with Scripture's many references to freedom, lest we assume that the kind of liberty valued in our society is the very same promised by God.

From and For

Freedom is a gift from our triune God. The apostle Paul gives thanks to God the Father because we have been set free from sin and become slaves to righteousness (Rom. 6:17–18). In John's Gospel, we read about the work of the Son: "So if the Son sets you free, you will be free indeed" (John 8:36). Paul declares, "For freedom Christ has set us free" (Gal. 5:1). And in 2 Corinthians, we are reminded that "where the Spirit of the Lord is, there is freedom" (2 Cor. 3:17). The Father sent the Son and Spirit, his two hands, into the world to break the chains of all the things that enslave us. It is for living a life of freedom that God has set us free.

From the small sampling of Scripture passages just cited, we might notice that freedom has at least two dimensions for Christians. There are some things we are set free *from* and things that we are set free *for*. In Acts 13:39, we hear Peter say that everyone who believes in Christ is "freed from everything from which you could not be freed by the law of Moses." The main bondage from which we are freed is that of sin, death, and judgment (Rom. 6:7, 18, 22; 8:1–2). We are free from bondage to customs and laws (Gal. 5:1). We, along with all creation, will be set free from our bondage to decay and corruption. And we are free from giving final allegiance to earthly governing authorities (1 Pet. 2:13–16). When Christians declare, "I have freedom in Christ," referring to their liberty concerning gray areas or human traditions, they are speaking the truth—but possibly only half the truth.

It is equally important to consider what we've been freed for—that is, the purpose for which we were set free. Paul writes, "But now that you have been set free from sin and have become slaves of God, the fruit you get leads to sanctification and its end, eternal life" (Rom. 6:22). The purpose of being set free from sin is to live sanctified lives, leading to the ultimate prize of eternal life. Elsewhere Paul adds, "For you were called to freedom, brothers. Only do not use your freedom as an opportunity for the flesh, but through love serve one another" (Gal. 5:13). And Peter writes, "Live as people who are free, not using your freedom as a cover-up for evil, but living as servants of God" (1 Pet. 2:16). In other words, we are set free in order to serve others in love. Our freedom in Christ is a freedom for others—God and his people.

Lords and Servants

One of the most famous statements regarding Christian freedom was penned by Martin Luther and includes both the *from* and *for* elements. He writes paradoxically,

> A Christian individual is a completely free lord of all, subject to none.
> A Christian individual is a completely dutiful servant of all, subject to all.[1]

On the surface, these statements do not sit well together, but Luther explains their biblical roots:

1 The following quotes are from Martin Luther, *The Freedom of a Christian, 1520: The Annotated Luther Study Edition*, ed. Timothy J. Wengert (Fortress, 2016), 10–25.

> For both are from the Apostle Paul, when he says in 1 Cor. 9[:19], "For though I am free with respect to all, I have made myself a slave to all" and in Rom. 13[:8], "Owe nothing to anyone except to love one another." But "love" by its very nature is dutiful and serves the one who is loved. The same was true of Christ who, although Lord of all, was nevertheless "born of a woman, born under the law" and who was at the same time free and slave, that is, at the same time "in the form of God" and "in the form of a slave."

A Christian is at one and the same time a free person and a servant, after the pattern set by our Lord. What it means to be free is to be justified by faith, free from having to establish a righteousness of our own through works. Even meditation, contemplation, or other efforts of the soul are of no benefit in achieving freedom as a Christian. "One thing and one thing alone is necessary for the Christian life, righteousness, and freedom," Luther writes, "and that is the most holy word of God, the Gospel of Christ." It is the gospel that we hear and believe and through which we are justified and set free from the burden of laws, not to mention condemnation.

Not only is the Christian a free lord of all through faith in Christ, but he is also a dutiful servant of all. This is where outward works come in. Good works are still required toward God and neighbor. But the motivation to produce good works is not the desire to attain righteousness and freedom. Rather, Luther writes,

> Since, therefore, works do not justify anyone and a person must be righteous before doing something good, these things are absolutely clear: that faith alone—because of the sheer mercy of God through Christ [given] in his word—properly

> and completely justifies and saves a person; and that no law is necessary for a Christian's salvation, since through faith one is free from every law and does everything that is done spontaneously, out of sheer freedom. Such a person seeks nothing for a payment or for salvation—already being satisfied and saved by God's grace from one's faith—but seeks only what pleases God.

This is such an important point about Christian freedom. Because we have been set free through faith, we no longer have to pursue good works as desperate slaves trying to meet a quota. Rather, having been set free, we seek only to please God through our service rather than pursue payment for our work. We love God and neighbor out of "sheer freedom," as Luther puts it, not as a way to get what we need most but as those who already have everything we need. In Christ, we have become free slaves, liberated from the burden of works and liberated for service to God and his people.

The Truth Will Set You Free

Luther's appeal to God's word as the source of freedom is echoed in our psalm. The psalmist exclaims,

> I will walk freely in an open place
> because I study your precepts. (Ps. 119:45 CSB)

God's precepts are given not as a way of confining or straitjacketing us but as a way of setting us free *from* sin and its effects and *for* blessing. Giving attention to God's word leads to freedom. As one commentator puts it, "As with a train, true liberty comes from staying on the tracks of obedience to God's instruction, not by going off the rails in an attempt to do as one pleases."[2] "Walking freely" comes from obedience to God's word.

In John's Gospel, Jesus turns to some Jews who "believed him"—not full-on disciples but those who were open and nonantagonistic—and tells them that they are slaves. At least, that is what he implies when he says to them, "If you abide in my word, you are truly my disciples, and you will know the truth, and the truth will set you free" (John 8:31–32). Only slaves need to be freed. For our purposes, it's noteworthy that Jesus says that the way to freedom—from the burden of the law, from sin, from custom, from themselves, from Satan—is to "abide" in his word. And the truth found in that word will set them free. Yet it is clear a few verses later that the one who sets us free is Jesus himself: "If the Son sets you free, you will be free indeed" (8:36). How does the Son, not to mention the Father and Spirit, set us free? By giving us his liberating word.

God's word brings us into contact with his justifying, sanctifying, conscience-cleansing, service-empowering, bond-breaking grace.

Bless Thou the truth, dear Lord, to me, to me,
As Thou didst bless the bread by Galilee;
Then shall all bondage cease, all fetters fall;
And I shall find my peace, my All in all.

MARY A. LATHBURY
"Break Thou the Bread of Life"
1877

2 Daniel J. Estes, *Psalms 73–150*, in The New American Commentary (B&H, 2019), 412.

16

The Gift of Life

I will never forget your precepts,
for by them you have given me life.

PSALM 119:93

ONE OF THE MOST FREQUENT word associations we find in Psalm 119 is between God's law and life. In our verse, the psalmist declares that God's precepts "have given me life." In several verses he prays, "Give me life according to your word" (119:25, 107) and "according to your promise" (119:154). Elsewhere, he expresses to the Lord,

> This is my comfort in my affliction,
> that your promise gives me life. (119:50)

It is worth asking what it means for the psalmist to receive life from the word and how it is that the word gives life.

Reviving the Soul

To receive life may simply mean that someone who is languishing or struggling in some way finds encouragement and strength. This is the sense we get from Psalm 19:7:

> The law of the LORD is perfect,
> reviving the soul.

To revive the soul is to have it refreshed or restored. One translator renders it as "bringing back the soul."[1] The law of the Lord brings the soul back from the brink of exhaustion or despair; it brings life in the face of looming death. This is also reflected in Psalm 119:50, where the psalmist derives comfort from the fact that God's "promise" gives him life. In other words, when we despair of life itself, somehow the word of God restores and renews us.

How does it do this? One clue is found in the term *promise* and its link to the phrase "according to your word," spread throughout Psalms. When the psalmist asks for God to do something according to his word, he is holding God to his revealed character and promises. For example, an episode that is branded in Israel's collective memory is when God revealed his glory to Moses after the golden calf fiasco. As he passes by Moses, he declares his "name":

> The LORD, the LORD, a God merciful and gracious, slow to anger, and abounding in steadfast love and faithfulness, keeping steadfast love for thousands, forgiving iniquity and transgression

1 J. H. Eaton, *The Psalms: A Historical and Spiritual Commentary with an Introduction and New Translation* (Continuum, 2005), 110.

> and sin, but who will by no means clear the guilty, visiting the iniquity of the fathers on the children and the children's children, to the third and the fourth generation. (Ex. 34:6–7)

After he reveals his name, he relents from his wrath, renews his covenantal commitment to Israel, and pledges his ongoing presence and care. What God shows and tells Moses—his merciful and gracious name—is recalled over and over again throughout the Old Testament (Num. 14:18; Neh. 9:17; Pss. 86:15; 103:8; 145:8; Joel 2:13; Jonah 4:2; Nah. 1:3). Every time these words are recalled, it reminds Israel of who God is and of who he will be for his people. For God to act according to his word is to act consistently with his self-declared character. In the midst of hardship or feelings of desertion, there is no greater comfort than God's steadfast love and faithfulness.

As an extension of his character, God makes a number of promises that give life to those in need of it. There are big covenantal promises like those made to Abraham and his descendants (Gen. 12:1–3) or David and his offspring (2 Sam. 7:14). There are also more universal promises, for example:

> The Lord is near to all who call on him,
> to all who call on him in truth. (Ps. 145:18 NIV)

> The Lord himself goes before you and will be with you; he will never leave you nor forsake you. Do not be afraid; do not be discouraged. (Deut. 31:8 NIV)

> Those who hope in the Lord
> will renew their strength.

They will soar on wings like eagles;
they will run and not grow weary,
they will walk and not be faint. (Isa. 40:31 NIV)

To the fearful, despairing, and weary, these scriptural promises are life-giving. They revive the soul according to God's word.

Regenerated by the Word

Another deep and profound way that the word of God gives life is by its role in regenerating us, or making us born again. While Jesus is clear that new birth is the work of the Holy Spirit (John 3:5), the New Testament reveals that the instrument for bringing about this new birth is God's word. In James's letter we read, "Of his own will he brought us forth by the word of truth" (James 1:18). Other versions translate "brought us forth" as "gave us birth" (e.g., CSB). Peter encourages believers to "love one another earnestly from a pure heart, *since you have been born again, not of perishable seed but of imperishable, through the living and abiding word of God*" (1 Pet. 1:22–23). What does it mean to be born again or regenerated?

In his usually picturesque way, Jonathan Edwards gives us a helpful working definition of regeneration. He writes,

> The work of the Spirit of God in regeneration is often in Scripture compared to the giving a new sense, giving eyes to see, and ears to hear, unstopping the ears of the deaf, and opening the eyes of them that were born blind, and turning from darkness unto light. And because this spiritual sense is immensely the

> most noble and excellent, and that without which all other principles of perception, and all our faculties are useless and vain; therefore the giving this new sense, with the blessed fruits and effects of it in the soul, is compared to a raising the dead, and to a new creation.[2]

One important writing within the Reformed tradition known as "the Leiden Synopsis" describes this new spiritual sense as "the circumcision of the heart, the conversion to God, the renewal of the Spirit, the sanctification of man, the new creation, and the first resurrection." This transformation affects every part of the soul that has been damaged by sin, such as our intellect, affections, and especially our will. Our intellect is "enlightened unto the knowledge of God and our Savior Jesus Christ," our affections are stirred to "hate sin and Satan, to love God and righteousness, and to hope for eternal life and the inheritance," and our will is renewed so that it is inclined toward spiritual good and begins to love and trust God.[3]

When addressing the question of how regeneration comes about, the "Synopsis" is emphatic that Christ—in his death and resurrection—and the Spirit are the ones who ultimately lie behind it. It goes on to say, however, that "the instrumental cause of this benefit is the Word of God, both that of the Law and that of the Gospel." In other words, the instrument the Spirit uses to apply the work of Christ to our lives is the word of God.

2 Jonathan Edwards, *Religious Affections*, ed. John E. Smith, vol. 2 of *The Works of Jonathan Edwards* (Yale University Press, 2009), 206.

3 The following quotes are from William Den Boer and Riemer A. Faber, eds., *Synopsis of a Purer Theology*, 2 vols., trans. Riemer A. Faber (Davenant, 2023), 2:372–76.

Following classic Reformation thought, the "Synopsis" claims that through the law we come to know our sinfulness and condemnation without which "we cannot possibly grasp the regeneration and repentance that bring salvation." Yet conviction regarding our lowly state is not enough to bring about regeneration. That's why the "Synopsis" adds,

> But it is through the Gospel and its promises that man conceives a godly sorrow, lifts up his downcast conscience to hope for forgiveness, and then makes Christ his own. He does so not only for the forgiveness of prior sins, but also for doing away with the old man and bringing to life the new one. For this reason, the Gospel is called "the ministry of the Spirit and of life" (2 Cor 3[:8–10]) and "the immortal seed of God that remains forever, through which we are born again" (1 Pet 1:23; James 1:18).

Becoming born again does not happen in a vacuum. Regeneration happens within the environment of the convicting and life-giving word of God. While Reformed writers will acknowledge that it could theoretically happen apart from the word—since God can do it however and whenever he pleases—it typically happens when the word is heard or read.

The Instrument of Life

All this theological language is helpful for understanding the role of God's word not only in bringing about regeneration but also in reviving our souls. Referring to the word of God as the "instrumental cause" of a new and renewed life does not insinuate that doing something like playing an audio Bible on repeat for background noise is the ideal environment in which to experience the Spirit's life-giving ministry. Instead, looking back to Psalm 119:93, the writer hints at the kind of Scripture engagement that tills the soil for the Spirit to act (this is something that will be addressed in more detail in the last chapter). The psalmist writes, "I will never forget your precepts"; in other words, he will regularly call them to mind. The word of God works to give life not when we are passive recipients of it but when we actively take it in and seek to understand it. It has to infiltrate our mind; it must stir things in our soul. The law has to engender an awareness of sin, the gospel an awareness of God's promises. The point is that receiving life from the Scriptures is not automatic, requiring nothing but the mere presence of the Bible in our lives. At the very least, our intellects must be engaged. There must be some measure of understanding if the word is going to do its good work. That's what the psalmist suggests when he writes,

> Your testimonies are righteous forever;
> give me understanding that I may live. (Ps. 119:144)

Life comes through understanding God's testimonies. If we want to experience life that is truly life, we must press in to know the Scriptures, God's good instrument for reviving our souls. The Spirit will take care of the rest.

Sing them over again to me,
Wonderful words of life;
Let me more of their beauty see,
Wonderful words of life;
Words of life and beauty
Teach me faith and duty.

Christ, the blessed one, gives to all
Wonderful words of life;
Sinner, list to the loving call,
Wonderful words of life;
All so freely given,
Wooing us to heaven.

Sweetly echo the gospel call,
Wonderful words of life;
Offer pardon and peace to all,
Wonderful words of life;
Jesus, only Savior,
Sanctify forever.

PHILIP P. BLISS
"Wonderful Words of Life"
1874

17

The Gift of Joy

The precepts of the Lord are right,
rejoicing the heart.

PSALM 19:8

I find my delight in your commandments,
which I love.

PSALM 119:47

WE HAVE A LITTLE TRADITION in our family that on each child's birthday, we go back and watch old videos of them "as kids." (They're still kids, in my opinion, even though they're teenagers now.) We have footage of them doing all sorts of things: holding church services in our living room when they were ages one, four, and five; playing peekaboo (or "teekpo," as one child puts it); asking and begging to get out of their rooms (too) early in the morning; putting on countless musical and dance performances; and many more. There is something so pure, so right about these blasts from the past. That's why every year, without fail, they fill me with so much joy and laughter.

Joy is a good thing. If the first question and answer of the Westminster Shorter Catechism is correct when it says that the chief goal of human existence is "to glorify God, and to enjoy him forever," then it's clear that we were made for joy. It is not merely something that we may passively receive from time to time—if we are so lucky. It is to be *pursued* if, in fact, it is "the chief end of man."

The question before us is always "In what do I find joy?" In other words, what is the source and object of my joy? The Westminster Shorter Catechism is not ambiguous on this question. Our joy must be found ultimately in God. God is the source. God is the object. This does not mean that I shouldn't find (or even pursue) joy in my kids' baby videos, but it does mean that my joy is to have a certain shape and orientation. It must be connected meaningfully to God himself.

Around the time that he wrote *Confessions*, Augustine also wrote a short book on how to interpret the Bible called *On Christian Teaching*. In it, he spends a surprisingly great deal of time reflecting on what it means to enjoy God (and other things). Fairly early in the book, he writes, "To enjoy something is to hold fast to it in love for its own sake. To use something is to apply whatever it may be to the purpose of obtaining what you love—if indeed it is something that ought to be loved."[1] Love and joy are bound together. We enjoy what we love for its own sake. We use, not abuse, whatever helps us love what

1 Augustine, *On Christian Teaching*, trans. R. P. H. Green, Oxford World's Classics (Oxford University Press, 2008), I.4.4 (9).

ought to be loved. Later on, he clarifies how all this relates to God. "By love," he writes, "I mean the impulse of one's mind to enjoy God on his own account and to enjoy oneself and one's neighbour on account of God."[2] God must be loved for his own sake; others must be loved—truly loved and truly enjoyed—as reflections of God's wisdom, beauty, and kindness. So, the answer to the first question of the catechism might be restated as "Man's chief end is to glorify God and to enjoy him, and everything in relation to him, forever." We are well within our rights to make joy the goal of our days, each and every morning.

Rejoicing the Heart

In one of our passages, notice how the psalmist brings together love and joy:

> I find my delight in your commandments,
>   which I love. (Ps. 119:47)

His love is defined by his delight. One gets the impression that the "chief end" of Psalm 119 is to encourage readers to enjoy and to love God's word and, in doing so, enjoy and love God himself. In several places, the psalmist declares how much he delights in God's word. God's statutes are the song in his heart (119:54). God's law is as delightful as "all riches" and "great spoil" (119:14, 162). The psalmist credits his perseverance in trials and hope for salvation to his delight in the law (119:92, 143, 174). His delight is an

2 Augustine, *On Christian Teaching*, 3.10.14 (76).

attitude of the heart that he brings to his engagement with God's word. Yet it is also the result of meditating on the law. Elsewhere in the Psalms, we read,

> The precepts of the Lord are right,
> rejoicing the heart. (Ps. 19:8)

The precepts of God, his instructions, are upright, and this leads to joy in the heart of the psalmist. Calvin sees the contrast here as between "the rectitude of the law and the crooked ways in which men entangle themselves when they follow their own understandings." He adds,

> We know how much every man is wedded to himself, and how difficult it is to eradicate from our minds the vain confidence of our own wisdom. It is therefore of great importance to be well convinced of this truth, that a man's life cannot be ordered aright unless it is framed according to the law of God, and that without this he can only wander in labyrinths and crooked bypaths.

Our delight flows from having a clear conscience, knowing that our lives are pleasing to God because they are ordered according to his law. Calvin concludes, "Those who take delight in committing sin procure for themselves abundant matter of sorrow; but the observance of the law of God, on the contrary, brings to man true joy."[3] The psalmist's heart overflows with pleasure in the law, and this pleasure leads to further engagement and obedience, which

3 John Calvin, *Commentary on the Book of Psalms*, trans. James Anderson, in *Calvin's Commentaries* (Baker, 2003), 1:320–21.

then results in further joy, and so on. Ultimately, his delight is in the covenant Lord, who graciously provides his good word for the benefit of his people.

Happy in God

Finding joy in and through God's word is a major lesson I've gleaned from one of my heroes in the faith, George Müller, a missionary and pastor in nineteenth-century England. He is most famous for his faith in God to provide for the needs of the many orphans he cared for in the city of Bristol. His method for providing for orphans was to raise money without ever asking anyone except God! Müller claimed that from the beginning of his ministry to the time of his death, God answered over fifty thousand prayer requests, thirty thousand of them within the same hour or day. In fact, through prayer alone, he was able to raise roughly $130 million (in today's money)![4]

Throughout his ministry, Müller shepherded a congregation (sometimes two congregations) of 1,200 people, distributed tracts and other Christian literature (for free) to millions of people, founded day schools that taught over 123,000 students over his lifetime, supported countless missionaries (including Hudson Taylor), built five orphanages that cared for over ten thousand children during his life, sparked a revival that impacted hundreds of thousands of people in the UK and Europe, and traveled to forty-two countries, preaching over five thousand times (between the ages of 70 and 87).[5]

4 Jim Elliff, introduction to *Autobiography of George Müller: A Million and a Half in Answer to Prayer* (Westminster Literature Resources, 2003), ix.

5 Roger Steer, *George Müller: Delighted in God* (Christian Focus, 1997), 188.

Müller was a remarkable man not only because of his outward productivity but also because of his walk with the Lord. In the middle years of his ministry, after being a Christian for quite some time, he made a discovery that transformed his spiritual life. And it had to do with how God's word and our joy intersect. Since it's best to hear it directly from Müller himself, I will quote him at length:

> It has recently pleased the Lord to teach me a truth, the benefit of which I have not lost. The point is this: I saw more clearly than ever that the first great and primary business to which I ought to attend every day was *to have my soul happy in the Lord.* The first thing to be concerned about was not how much I might serve the Lord, how I might glorify the Lord, but how I might get my soul into a happy state, and how my inner man might be nourished. For I might seek to set the truth before the unconverted, I might seek to benefit believers, I might seek to relieve the distressed, I might in other ways seek to behave myself as it becomes a child of God in this world; and yet, not being happy in the Lord, and not being nourished and strengthened in my inner man day by day, all this might not be attended to in a right spirit.

His former practice was to begin the morning in prayer. He often found himself, however, distracted or his mind wandering. In the process of prayer, he derived little comfort or encouragement even after praying for large stretches of time. It took a lot of time before he began "really to pray." Therefore, rather than beginning his day in prayer, he began it by meditating on the word of God and, in doing so, he received comfort, encouragement, rebuke, and instruction. He writes that his heart, while meditating, was "brought into experiential communion with the Lord":

> I began therefore to meditate on the New Testament from the beginning, early in the morning. The first thing I did, after having asked in a few words the Lord's blessing upon his precious word, was, to begin to meditate on the word of God, searching as it were into every verse, to get blessing out of it; not for the sake of the public ministry of the word, not for the sake of preaching on what I had meditated upon, but for the sake of obtaining food for my own soul. The result I have found to be almost always this, that after a very few minutes my soul has been led to confession, or to thanksgiving, or to intercession, or to supplication; so that, though I did not give myself to *prayer*, but to *meditation*, yet it turned almost immediately more or less into prayer. The result of this is, that there is always a good deal of confession, thanksgiving, supplication, or intercession mingled with my meditation, and that my inner man almost invariably is even sensibly nourished and strengthened, and that by breakfast time, with rare exceptions, I am in a peaceful if not happy state of heart.

Prayer—deep, joyful, heartfelt prayer—flowed from meditating on Scripture. Müller certainly does not discount prayer, but he wants to make it clear that the fount of joy is God's word. He concludes,

> By the blessing of God I ascribe to this mode the help and strength which I have had from God to pass in peace through

> deeper trials, in various ways, than I had ever had before; and after having now above fourteen years tried this way, I can most fully, in the fear of God, commend it. How different, when the soul is refreshed and made happy early in the morning, from what it is when, without spiritual preparation, the service, the trials, and the temptations of the day come upon one![6]

The goal of each day, for Müller, was to get himself as joyful in God as possible. Yet his pathway to daily joy was through careful, deliberate, patient, and prayerful meditation on God's word until his heart felt "comforted, encouraged, warned, reproved, instructed," until his heart was "brought into experiential communion with the Lord." This wasn't a vague mystical experience. He pored intently over the Scriptures, seeking to get a blessing from them that would be food for his soul and *not* primarily for his ministry. After his heart was nourished by God's truth, he then prayed for things that came to mind in his reading of the word. All this was done before embarking on his long day of ministry.

May we make it our daily ambition to be happy—exceedingly joyful—in the Lord.

> Oh, how I love Thy holy law!
> 'Tis daily my delight;
> And thence my meditations draw
> Divine advice by night.

6 Müller, *Autobiography*, 152–54 (emphasis original).

My waking eyes prevent the day
To meditate Thy Word;
My soul with longing melts away
To hear Thy Gospel, Lord.

How doth Thy Word my heart engage!
How well employ my tongue!
And in my toilsome pilgrimage
Yields me a heavenly song.

When nature sinks, and spirits droop,
Thy promises of grace
Are pillars to support my hope,
And there I write Thy praise.

ISAAC WATTS
"Oh, How I Love Thy Holy Law"
1740

18

The Gift of Wisdom

Your commandment makes me wiser than my enemies,
for it is ever with me.

PSALM 119:98

IT ALWAYS AMAZES ME how much the book of Psalms talks about enemies. A songbook about enemies seems too serious, negative, and unhappy, especially when you compare it to the typical worship set that we might get on a Sunday morning. Here's a small sampling of some early songs in Israel's enemy-laden hymnbook:

Arise, O LORD!
Save me, O my God!
For you strike all my enemies on the cheek;
you break the teeth of the wicked. (Ps. 3:7)

Lead me, O LORD, in your righteousness
because of my enemies;
make your way straight before me. (5:8)

All my enemies shall be ashamed and greatly troubled;
they shall turn back and be put to shame in a moment.
(6:10)

If I have repaid my friend with evil
or plundered my enemy without cause,
let the enemy pursue my soul and overtake it,
and let him trample my life to the ground
and lay my glory in the dust. *Selah*

Arise, O Lord, in your anger;
lift yourself up against the fury of my enemies. (7:4–6)

While our worship services might contain the odd song that mentions Jesus's conquering of the enemy, songs about the wiles and schemes of our enemies or about our oppression at their hands are not common themes.

Noticing this theme in the Psalms sometimes leads me to ask, "Do I have any enemies? Should I have any enemies? Should Christians have enemies? If so, who or what are they?"

The tidiest answer might be to say that our enemies are only spiritual and not human (Eph. 6:10–12). But this answer ignores the whole Old Testament as well as several passages in the New Testament that speak about human enemies of Christ, of Christians, and of the cross (e.g., Ps. 3:7; Matt. 10:36; Acts 13:10; Phil. 3:18).

God and his people have real enemies. The Puritan preacher Thomas Manton writes, "By enemies is not to be understood those only that were troublesome to himself [the psalmist], but those who were an opposite party to God, who opposed themselves against God and godliness."[1] They are those who oppose God's ways and anyone who aligns themselves with these ways. True, the ultimate enemy is the evil one, but there are also human enemies who oppose God and his faithful ones.

Wiser Than My Foes

This brings us to our passage. The psalmist is very aware of his enemies. We are not privy to what exactly their schemes are. The psalmist simply exclaims,

> Your commandment makes me wiser than my enemies,
> for it is ever with me. (Ps. 119:98)

This is not thinly-veiled conceit rooted in the psalmist's inflated sense of self. Rather, he insinuates that his enemies foolishly think they are wise in their opposition to him and, presumably, to God. He is mindful that there are always two kinds of wisdom at work in his circumstances: wisdom from below and wisdom from above. James describes the former as "earthly, unspiritual, demonic," taking the form of "jealousy and selfish ambition . . . and every vile practice" (James 3:14–16). Wisdom from above is "pure" and "peaceable," and produces "a harvest of righteousness" (3:17–18). These opponents ignore God's wisdom and only display an earthly wisdom that will lead to their demise. The psalmist, however, keeps God's commandments close to his heart. He is able to overcome their schemes because of the

1 Thomas Manton, "Sermon 156, Ps 119:139," in *The Complete Works of Thomas Manton*, 22 vols. (J. Nisbet, 1870–1875), 8:465.

wisdom granted by God's word. Matthew Henry helpfully summarizes the point:

> By studying and practising God's commandments, and making them his rule, he learnt to *behave himself wisely in all his ways*. . . . He outwitted his enemies; God, by these means, made him wiser to baffle and defeat their designs against him. . . . By keeping the commandments we secure God on our side and make him our friend, and therein are certainly wiser than those that make him their enemy. By keeping the commandments we preserve in ourselves that peace and quiet of mind which our enemies would rob us of, and so are wise for ourselves, wiser than they are for themselves, for this world as well as for the other.[2]

Mister Worldly-Wiseman, Our Frenemy

While we do indeed have real, concrete enemies, both human and spiritual, it is helpful to expand the category of adversaries to include all ideas and ways of thinking that set themselves above God's wisdom. The apostle Paul, speaking of the constant battle in which we find ourselves as Christians, writes,

> For though we walk in the flesh, we are not waging war according to the flesh. For the weapons of our warfare are not of the flesh but have divine power to destroy strongholds. We destroy arguments and every lofty opinion raised against the knowledge of God, and take every thought captive to obey Christ, being

2 Matthew Henry, *Job to Song of Solomon*, vol. 3, in *Commentary on the Whole Bible*, https://ccel.org/, comment on Psalm 119:98–100.

> ready to punish every disobedience, when your obedience is complete. (2 Cor. 10:3–6)

Notice how Paul describes his enemy. While he speaks about real human opponents, he also speaks about what they espouse. His enemies include "arguments and every lofty opinion" that set themselves up against the knowledge of God. What is intriguing but also potentially beguiling is that oftentimes our enemy does not come in the form of open hostility. Our enemy, as in the case of the Corinthian church and the false teachers Paul opposes, may come under the guise of a friend.

There is a poignant episode in John Bunyan's *Pilgrim's Progress* that captures the subtle allure of ideas contrary to divine wisdom. Those familiar with the story know that Christian, the main character, is on a journey from the City of Destruction to the Celestial City to find someone who can remove the burden of his sins from him. Early in his journey, after struggling his way through the Slough of Despond, a swamp of despair and doubt, he sees in the distance a finely dressed man coming toward him. The man is Mr. Worldly-wiseman from the town called Carnal Policy. He's heard of Christian's journey from the City of Destruction and, feeling concern for Christian's burden, offers him some counsel: "I would advise you to get rid of your Burden quickly," he says. "You'll never have peace of mind until you do, and you'll never enjoy the blessings God has given you until then either." This sounds like music to Christian's ears, but he is reticent to take Wiseman's advice since he was advised earlier by Evangelist that the only way to have his burdens removed was to journey to the

Celestial City. Mister Worldly-wiseman, indignant at Evangelist's counsel, responds,

> There is not a more dangerous and troublesome way in all the world than the one that he steered you toward. And that is what you will find if you allow yourself to be led by his counsel. I can tell that you've already had some trouble, for I can see the dirt of the Slough of Despond on you. That Slough is only the beginning of the sorrows that come to those who take this way. Listen to me, for I am older than you. If you take this way you will likely meet with fatigue, pain, hunger, dangers, nakedness, sword, lions, dragons, darkness, and, in a word, death. This is the truth, and it has been confirmed by many testimonies. Should a man be so careless as to throw his life away by giving heed to a stranger?[3]

Christian is undeterred. All the hardships in the world are worth it if only he can have the burden removed. So Mr. Worldly-wiseman continues his interrogation. He asks the pilgrim how he first received his burden. Christian reports that the burden came after reading the Book (Scripture). To this Mr. Worldly-wiseman responds,

> I thought so. And it has happened to you just like to other weak people who, meddling with things beyond their understanding, fall into the same mental confusion and obsessive behavior as you have. This can only break a man down, and I can perceive

3 The following quotes are from John Bunyan, *The Pilgrim's Progress*, retold by Cheryl V. Ford (Tyndale, 2016), 13–16.

> this is the case with you. These people take off on desperate ventures seeking to receive something they know nothing about.

Christian insists he knows exactly what he's searching for: freedom from his burden. This provokes Mr. Worldly-wiseman's question:

> But why do you seek for freedom in this way, seeing that it's so dangerous? If you had the patience to listen, I could direct you to what you are looking for without the dangers that you'll encounter by going this way. . . . Instead of those dangers, you'll find abundant safety, friendship, and contentment.

Intrigued by this prospect, Christian asks, "Please reveal this secret to me." Mister Worldly-wiseman obliges,

> Well, a short distance from here there is a Village named Morality. In this Village lives a man named Legality. This man has sound judgment and a very good reputation. He has skill in helping people like yourself get such burdens off their shoulders. . . . If he is not at home himself, he has a son, an impressive young man named Civility. He can help you just as well as the old man. You will be able to find relief from your Burden there. . . . All you need to make your life happy is there, and you will live by honest neighbors who are successful and of a good reputation.

Christian is convinced by this counsel and so seeks directions to Legality's home. Mister Worldly-wiseman points to a high hill where the man lives. So Christian deviates from his original path and journeys to Legality's house. As he approaches the hill, he notices that it is far steeper than he'd anticipated. And the path that he's on has a dangerous looking overhang that Christian fears might fall on him. He also notices that his burden is now heavier than before he met Mr. Worldly-wiseman. Christian is stuck, frozen in fear. The episode concludes, "Now he was sorry that he had ever taken Mr. Worldly-wiseman's advice."

The allegory is fairly straightforward. Christian is burdened by sin, and he knows that the only way to be relieved of sin is by having the King remove it. Instead, Mr. Worldly-wiseman assures him that choosing a life of morality—obeying the law (Legality) or being a well-mannered citizen (Civility)—is enough to lift the burden. He looks down on those who take the Scriptures seriously and are willing to heed its diagnoses and remedies. In his view, it is better to choose a life of ease than the hard road that Scripture offers. According to Bunyan, this is the wisdom of the world, and it only leads to a greater burden or even death. God's path, however difficult, is always the way to life and freedom.

Confounding Worldly Wisdom

The apostle Paul speaks forcefully about the power of God's word to make us wiser than the world. In 1 Corinthians 1, he weaves together the gospel and the power of God: "For the message of the cross is foolishness to those who are perishing, but to us who are being saved it is the power of God" (1 Cor. 1:18 NIV). Paul declares that God has made foolish the wisdom of the world—teachers of the law and philosophers alike. Then he quotes Isaiah:

> I will destroy the wisdom of the wise;
> the intelligence of the intelligent I will frustrate.
> (1 Cor. 1:19 NIV; cf. Isa. 29:14)

God destroys the wisdom of the wise. Yet according to Paul, he does this through "the foolishness of what was preached" so that *through the gospel* we can experience Christ as the power and wisdom of God. Both God and his word are the source of world-confounding wisdom.

Paul is aware that God's wisdom appears as foolishness to those who don't receive it. But he wants to make sure that we know that "the foolishness of God is wiser than human wisdom, and the weakness of God is stronger than human strength" (1 Cor. 1:25 NIV). This is where the rubber meets the road for many of us. Do we believe that the word of God gives us wisdom that is greater than what the *New York Times*, *Washington Post*, or Fox News can provide? Do we believe that it gives us greater wisdom than Christianity's cultured despisers? Whether it's the message of the cross, a word of correction, or a word of encouragement, God's word is wiser and makes *us* wiser than the wisdom of the world. Through it, we gain access to Christ "who has become for us wisdom from God—that is, our righteousness, holiness and redemption" (1:30 NIV).

> And though this world, with devils filled,
> should threaten to undo us,
> we will not fear, for God has willed

his truth to triumph through us.
The prince of darkness grim,
we tremble not for him;
his rage we can endure,
for lo! his doom is sure;
one little word shall fell him.

MARTIN LUTHER
"A Mighty Fortress"
1529

19

The Gift of Righteousness

Therefore the wicked will not stand in the judgment,
nor sinners in the congregation of the righteous.

PSALM 1:5

Righteous are you, O LORD,
and right are your rules. . . .

Seven times a day I praise you
for your righteous rules.

PSALM 119:137, 164

RIGHTEOUSNESS COMES through God's word. Righteousness does not come through God's law. Both of these statements are true, even if they seem contradictory at first glance. If we return to Psalm 1, which in some way has been the basis of everything we've said thus far, we see the first sentence affirmed. The blessed man who delights in the law and meditates on it all day is contrasted with the wicked man who rejects God's counsel. The godly man bears fruit, while the wicked does not. The latter is like chaff that is blown away by the wind. Because the wicked man refuses to joyfully receive the law, the psalmist warns,

> Therefore the wicked will not stand in the judgment,
> nor sinners in the congregation of the righteous. (Ps. 1:5)

It is implied that the blessed man *will* stand in the congregation of the righteous. He will be numbered among them, as the following verse confirms when it calls him "righteous" (1:6). The key? Delighting in the *law*. In other words, righteousness comes through God's word.

On the other hand, the apostle Paul is emphatic that "the righteousness of God has been manifested apart from the law" (Rom. 3:21) and that "if righteousness were through the law, then Christ died for no purpose" (Gal. 2:21). Obedience to God's law is presented by Paul as a hindrance to righteousness (Rom. 10:1–4; Phil. 3:8–9). True righteousness from God comes along a different path.

The word of God is both necessary and a roadblock to righteousness. How can this be?

Two Kinds of Righteousness

Early in his ministry, Martin Luther preached a sermon on Philippians 2:5–6 in which he explored different ways of thinking about righteousness from a biblical perspective. He begins, "There are two kinds of Christian righteousness, just as man's sin is of two kinds." He calls the first kind of righteousness "alien"—that is, the righteousness of another—"instilled from without." In other words, this is the righteousness of Christ by which we are justified through faith. This first kind of righteousness is an immeasurable gift that comes through our union with Christ. Luther writes,

> This is an infinite righteousness, and one that swallows up all sins in a moment, for it is impossible that sin should exist in Christ. On the contrary, he who trusts in Christ exists in Christ; he is one with Christ, having the same righteousness as he. It is therefore impossible that sin should remain in him.

Then comes the key statement:

> This righteousness is primary; it is the basis, the cause, the source of all our own actual righteousness. For this is the righteousness given in place of the original righteousness lost in Adam. It accomplishes the same as that original righteousness would have accomplished; rather, it accomplishes more.

For Luther, alien righteousness is both imputed and imparted. What this means is that in Christ, we have received a righteous standing, having all our sins swallowed up by his own righteousness. But we have also been imparted with a new righteousness that is meant to grow over time. But the point for Luther is that this righteousness comes from outside of us and is accessed through faith in Christ.

The second kind of righteousness is our own "proper righteousness," in which we gradually become righteous in ourselves. Luther explains, "This righteousness goes on to complete the first for it ever strives to do away with the old Adam and to destroy the body of sin. . . . It does God's will, living soberly with self, justly with neighbor, devoutly toward God." Perhaps by the word "complete" he means that what we are in Christ by faith, we become more fully by love. "Proper righteousness" is not self-generated but rather is the product, fruit, and consequence of the alien righteousness received through faith. In a rich image that describes the relationship between the two kinds of righteousness, Luther writes, "Therefore through the first righteousness arises the voice of the bridegroom who says to the soul, 'I am yours,' but through the second comes the voice of the bride who answers, 'I am yours.' Then the marriage is consummated."[1] Faith connects us to the bridegroom and all that belongs to him. In that relationship, we commit to live *for* the bridegroom and *like* the bridegroom—in love of God and neighbor.

The Object of Faith

This foray into Luther helps to highlight two ways that the word of God intersects with our righteousness. The first has to do with the relationship between the word and faith. Luther defines faith as "nothing else than believing what God promises and reveals."[2] He will add that without the word there can be no faith. Therefore, when it comes to alien righteousness, God's word of promise in the gospel is absolutely essential. Without that word, there is no faith; without faith there is no righteousness. In another sense, however, God's word—as in the law, or obedience to God's

1 Martin Luther, "Two Kinds of Righteousness," in *Career of the Reformer 1*, vol. 31 of *Luther's Works* (Fortress, 1979), 297–300.

2 Martin Luther, "Proceedings at Augsburg," in *Career of the Reformer 1*, 270–71.

commands—is not a prerequisite to alien righteousness. This righteousness does not come through obedience to God's word but only through union with Christ by faith. It is a gift. Thus when it comes to alien righteousness, God's word is essential but applied wrongly can be a hindrance to righteousness.

The second kind of righteousness is characterized by putting to death the flesh, loving our neighbor, and fearing God. As in the case of alien righteousness, this righteousness is dependent on God's word. When Moses was preparing the people of Israel to enter the promised land, he speaks these words to them:

> And the LORD commanded us to do all these statutes, to fear the LORD our God, for our good always, that he might preserve us alive, as we are this day. And it will be righteousness for us, if we are careful to do all this commandment before the LORD our God, as he has commanded us. (Deut. 6:24–25)

Moses makes clear that the emblem and evidence of their righteousness is their careful observance of the gracious commands God gave them. No commands, no righteousness. In their case, the law is at the center of their covenantal arrangement with God. They show themselves to be his people—already redeemed by grace—by their adherence to his commands. Their righteousness—that is, their proper reflection of the Lord's own righteousness—comes through obedience to the righteous commands of God.

In Luther's sermon, he places the example of Christ at the center of this second kind of righteousness. Christ is the pattern and the goal of our righteousness. We are to be conformed to his likeness. This is all true, especially as we ponder righteousness on this side of the cross and resurrection. We can go as far as saying that righteousness is about being *in* Christ and *like* Christ. But when we pause and ask, "Who is Christ, and where can I catch glimpses of his example?" we are always cast back to the Scriptures. God's word paints the only authoritative and trustworthy portrait of Christ we have. In Scripture, we see a Christ

- who loves God's law and is well versed in it at an early age (Luke 2:46–48);
- who submits to his parents (Luke 2:51);
- whose food is to do the Father's will, even to the point of death (Matt. 26:39; John 4:34);
- who is compassionate toward the masses of lost people (Matt. 9:36);
- who laments over Jerusalem (Matt. 23:37);
- who heals countless people, body and soul (Matt 4:23; 15:30; Mark 5:34);
- who serves even those who would betray him (John 13:10–12); and
- who suffers and gives his life as a ransom for many (Mark 10:45).

This indeed is true righteousness. But this pattern of life is made known to us in the Scriptures. When the Bible calls us to be imitators of Christ, it is not the Christ of our own imaginings that we are called to mimic. Instead, it is the Jesus of the apostles' preaching and captured for all time in the New Testament. So even if we were to limit actual righteousness to being like Christ, we would still find ourselves wholly dependent on God's word. Yet actual righteousness involves living out the whole counsel of God as those in Christ, in faith and love toward God. We need all that God has given us in the Scriptures—both Old and New Testaments—in order to walk uprightly before him. Like Israel, "it will be righteousness for us, if we are careful to do" (Deut. 6:25) all that God has revealed concerning his desires for us as his people.

The Righteous Circle

Throughout Psalm 119, the writer is emphatic that the root and standard of righteousness is God himself. In one of our passages, we read,

> Righteous are you, O LORD,
> and right are your rules. (Ps. 119:137)

The psalmist sees a connection between the righteousness of God and the rightness of his law. In another one of our passages, the psalmist declares,

> Seven times a day I praise you
> for your righteous rules. (119:164)

From the heart of a righteous God come his righteous rules. Through the righteous laws, we come to know the righteous one, Jesus, and through union with him are declared righteous. But then the righteous one directs us back to his word and empowers us to obey it and, thus, live righteous lives before him. This is the circle of righteousness. It begins and ends with God and has his word right at the heart of everything. Thank God for this inexpressible gift!

O Lord, Thy perfect righteousness
is in Thy judgments shown;
in Thy unchanging faithfulness
Thy truth Thou hast made known.

Because Thy foes forget Thy law
my soul is greatly stirred;
Thy servant loves the purity
of Thy most holy Word.

Though I am humble and despised,
I strive Thy will to do;
eternal is Thy righteousness,
and all Thy law is true.

Delight amid distress and pain
do Thy commandments give;
Thy word is righteous evermore,
teach me that I may live.

AUTHOR UNKNOWN
"O Lord, Thy Perfect Righteousness"
1912

20
The Gift of Hope

Never take the word of truth from my mouth,
for I hope in your judgments. . . .

Remember your word to your servant;
you have given me hope through it.

PSALM 119:43, 49 CSB

WHEN I WAS an unbelieving teenager, I wondered a lot about the purpose of life. At the time, I had big dreams of making a bunch of money, living the fabulous life, and being successful in this world. But then I started to ask, "Where will all the stuff that I'll accumulate go when I die? Where will *I* go when I die?" Growing up in a non-Christian home and having no exposure to Scripture and Christian teaching, I concluded that my destiny was nothingness—pure emptiness, blackness, nonexistence. This was such a troubling thought to me. I couldn't often bear it. I would sometimes get up from bed at night and wander around the house, trying to distract myself from those thoughts. I was one of the Gentiles that Paul describes as "having no hope and without God in the world" (Eph. 2:12)—that is, until I received a King James Bible on my eighteenth birthday and, soon after, encountered the one who says, "I am the resurrection and the life" (John 11:25).

Very few things capture the heart of the Christian faith more than hope. The apostle Paul claims that our hope in the resurrection makes Christianity what it is: "If Christ has not been raised, your faith is futile" (1 Cor. 15:17). He goes on to say that Christians would be the most pitiful people if our hope was anchored solely to this life (15:19). A. W. Tozer is correct when he writes, "Hope is the drift and direction of the whole Bible. It is the music of the whole Bible. It is the heartbeat, the pulse, the atmosphere of the whole Bible."[1]

What is hope? There are at least three ways we commonly use the word *hope*:

1. A desire for something good in the future ("I hope we win tomorrow").
2. Something in the future that we desire ("My hope is that mom gets home soon").
3. The reason for thinking that our desire may indeed be fulfilled ("Catching this train is our only hope of arriving on time").

John Piper points out that while these senses of hope are all found in Scripture, they lack a particular element of the full biblical picture. Each of the above is characterized by uncertainty, while biblical hope

1 A. W. Tozer, *The Tozer Pulpit: Selections from His Pulpit Ministry*, ed. Gerald B. Smith, 2 vols. (Christian Publications, 1994), 1:153.

is characterized by a kind of certainty. He defines biblical hope as "a confident expectation and desire for something good in the future."[2] Hope is anchored to the future. It is rooted in the character of the God who makes good promises. If God is who he declares and shows himself to be—wise, all-powerful, faithful, and kind—then we can have confidence that what he says he will do. He *will* certainly do.

As the people of this God, we are creatures of hope. Paul prays earnestly that we "may know what is the hope to which he has called [us]" (Eph. 1:18) and that the God of hope would fill us in such a way "that by the power of the Holy Spirit" we would "abound in hope" (Rom. 15:13). We hope for our own transformation and glory (Rom. 5:2; Gal. 5:5; Col. 1:27). We hope for deliverance from trials (2 Cor. 1:10), to not be ashamed in our service to Christ (Phil. 1:20), for our righteousness (Gal. 5:5), salvation (1 Thess. 5:8), eternal life (Titus 1:2; 3:7), and for "the appearing of the glory of our great God and Savior Jesus Christ" (Titus 2:13). We even mourn differently because of our hope. We're told not to "grieve as others do who have no hope" (1 Thess. 4:13). Why? Because we believe that Jesus Christ rose from the dead and will raise everyone that belongs to him (4:14). Peter connects our "apologetics" to hope when he tells believers to be "prepared to make a defense to anyone who asks you for a reason for the hope that is in you" (1 Pet. 3:15). Hope is, as Tozer says, the heartbeat of Scripture. But how do we get it?

Like all aspects of the Christian life, hope is something that originates in God. The apostle Paul writes that when we were saved, we were brought into the Christian hope (Rom. 8:24). Even better, Peter says that God "has *caused* us to be born again to a living hope

2 John Piper, "What Is Hope?," Desiring God, April 6, 1986, https://www.desiringgod.org/.

through the resurrection of Jesus Christ from the dead" (1 Pet. 1:3). We are ushered into hope by the hope-giving act of God raising Jesus from the dead. The fullness of new life that Christ experiences is ours now in part, but we await its fullness. All this is from God.

Troubled into Hope

Hope is also produced by tribulation. In Romans 5, Paul presents what might be seen as a hope production line. He writes, "We rejoice in our sufferings, knowing that suffering produces endurance, and endurance produces character, and character produces hope" (Rom. 5:3–4). The first stage of the production line has suffering joined with faith to produce patient endurance. Those who have patiently endured trials will have proven character—a sense of solidity that comes from experiencing God's provision and care. This experience of God's fatherly provision strengthens hope in God's continued care. Calvin summarizes,

> The saints, therefore, through forbearance experience the fact that God, when there is need, provides the assistance that he has promised. Thence, also, is their hope strengthened, inasmuch as it would be the height of ingratitude not to expect that in time to come God's truthfulness will be as constant and firm as they have already experienced it to be.[3]

Suffering does not produce hope automatically. Suffering could produce murmuring and complaining, poor character, and hopelessness. We must remember that these desired effects—patience,

3 John Calvin, *Institutes of the Christian Religion*, ed. John T. McNeill, trans. Ford Lewis Battles, 2 vols., Library of Christian Classics 20–21 (Westminster John Knox, 2006), 3.6.3.

character, hope—are the work of the Spirit using suffering as the means for producing these fruits.

Reminded into Hope

The idea of God using means to produce hope brings us to our passage. Our verse reads,

> Remember your word to your servant;
> you have given me hope *through* it. (Ps. 119:49 CSB)

The word spoken to the psalmist is the thing through which hope comes. Hope is an end; the word is the means to that end. In other words, the word of God produces hope. The apostle Paul clarifies the connection: "For whatever was written in former days was written for our instruction, that through endurance and through the encouragement of the Scriptures we might have hope" (Rom. 15:4). He says explicitly that the way Scripture generates hope is by the encouragements it gives—whether by God's promises or by the record of his acts in former days. God's word generates hope by recollecting; we are reminded into hope.

This is especially important to grasp before or as we find ourselves in trying circumstances. In the crucible of suffering, we are prone to lose perspective. We easily forget the promises of God or his powerful deeds of deliverance or even the handful of crystal-clear ways he has shown up in our lives. But Scripture helps us remember; it brings back to our consciousness the truth that we are not alone and that God is a willing, able, and present help in our time of trouble. Scripture is God's graciously given memory bank for when our memories fail us.

Hoped into Hope

Hope is also a verb. It is something we do and not just something we possess. Our other verse reads,

> Never take the word of truth from my mouth,
> for I hope in your judgments. (Ps. 119:43 CSB)

In this case, God's "judgments" or "rules" (ESV) are the focus of the psalmist's hope. He places his hope in God's law. In other words, the very same Scriptures that help to produce hope become the object of our hope. This theme is repeated throughout Psalm 119:

> Remember your word to your servant,
> in which you have made me hope. (119:49)

> Those who fear you shall see me and rejoice,
> because I have hoped in your word. (119:74)

> My soul longs for your salvation;
> I hope in your word. (119:81)

> You are my hiding place and my shield;
> I hope in your word. (119:114)

> I rise before dawn and cry for help;
> I hope in your words. (119:147)

This pattern should not surprise us given the intimate connection between God, the promisor, and his words of promise. The very one who gives us new birth into hope and something to hope for also gives us his words as a record and reminder of the hope he offers.

When Scripture says, "Hope in God" (e.g., Pss. 42:5, 11; 43:5), it may as well say, "Hope in God's word!" The Scriptures present to us a faithful God who has acted on behalf of his people in the past and will continue to work on behalf of those who are in Christ. If you want to know hope, acquaint yourself with the hope-giving word that comes from the mouth of the God of hope.

God, you're my everlasting hope,
I lean upon your truth;
your hands have held my childhood up,
and strengthened all my youth;

Still has my life new wonders seen
unfolding every year;
behold, my days that yet remain,
I trust them to your care.

Then, in the history of my age,
when others view my days,
they'll read your love on every page,
in every line, your praise.

ISAAC WATTS
"The Aged Saint's Reflection and Hope"
1719

Epilogue

Opening the Gift

THIS BOOK OF MEDITATIONS is meant to be just that: meditations, reflections on God's many-splendored kindness in giving his word. The goal is to simply fuel our love and appreciation for all that God's word is to us and all that God wants to be for us through his word. My main emphasis throughout the book is that the mere presence of God's word is a gift. While it may seem like something he owes us or just natural to the Creator-creature relationship, the fact that God would speak so as to be understood is an astonishing grace. Yet as in the case of many gifts, the joys and benefits of the gift are not experienced unless it is opened by the recipient. In other words, God's gift calls for a particular response.

Not only does Psalm 119 and its related psalms present the gift of Scripture and the other gifts that come through it, but they also teach us how to "open" those gifts by the ways we approach and respond to God's word. Opening the gift of God's word requires certain heart postures and certain practices. The psalmist experienced (or hoped to experience) the many benefits of Scripture because his heart and habits were oriented rightly toward it. In closing this book of meditations, let us reflect on some of the attitudes and actions revealed in Psalm 119 that help open the door to experiencing the gifts of Scripture in greater measure.

Postures

Delight

The most prominent posture toward God's law that we find in Psalm 119 is delight. In an earlier chapter, we reflected on joy and delight as benefits bestowed on us through God's word, but here it is worth taking note of how delight is a posture toward Scripture that opens up its benefits to us.

The psalmist delights in God's law as in "all riches" and "great spoil" (119:14; 162). One reason for such high praise and pleasure may be found in the function that the law plays: It is a trustworthy counselor (119:24). Delight is the opposite of forgetfulness or neglect (119:16). Delight is also a posture of the heart that puts the psalmist in a position to receive God's personal moral instruction and guidance (119:35). Delight is rooted in a love for God's commandments, and it overflows in reverence and meditation (119:47–48), the latter of which we will address shortly. Those who delight in God's word are the opposite of those whose hearts are "callous and unfeeling" (119:70 NIV; "fat and gross" NRSV).

A delighting heart is tender and receptive, open to God's comfort and rebuke. Delight is expressed in singing God's law (119:54, 172) and in raising our hands in worship toward it (119:48). Delighting in God's law is the natural posture of those who understand what they have received. One of the most appropriate ways to approach Scripture is to take delight in it not as a rigid rule book to be followed (although it does have rules) but as a gift to be received with joy from a delighted Author. In fact, if we want to experience more fully the gifts and delights of Scripture, joyful praise of it may be the best route. Perhaps this is what C. S. Lewis was getting at when he concludes, "I think we delight to praise what we enjoy because the praise not merely expresses but completes the enjoyment; it is its appointed consummation."[1]

Love

Closely related to delight is the love the psalmist declares for God's word. He writes,

> For I find my delight in your commandments,
> which I love. (Ps. 119:47)

At least ten times in Psalm 119, he declares his love for the law. He contrasts love with double-mindedness (119:113), suggesting that love means being fully devoted to God's law. He loves God's commands more than fine gold (119:127). The value of gold is tied up in what it can provide for us—security, influence, pleasure. The psalmist holds that God's word provides all those things and more and, therefore, is a more worthy object of love. He loves God's promises because they have proven true in his life as well as others' (119:140). The psalmist loves God's law because it is truthful and upright (119:163) and able to keep him from stumbling (119:165).

1 C. S. Lewis, *Reflections on the Psalms* (Fount, 1978), 79–81.

The heart is always the issue when it comes to how we approach God's word. At the beginning of his letter to the Philippians, Paul prays for the church "that your love will keep on growing in knowledge and every kind of discernment" (Phil. 1:9 CSB). Love precedes knowledge; knowledge requires love. If we want to reap the full benefits of God's word, we must attend to our hearts. We become what we love. So let's pray like Paul that our love would abound more and more for the Scriptures so that we will become more like the God that they reveal.

Faith and Hope

"Now hope that is seen is not hope. For who hopes for what he sees?" (Rom. 8:24). When the apostle Paul wrote these words, he was highlighting a central feature of hope. It is an unrealized promise—but a promise that is sure to be realized. It is holding on by faith to the promise of a better future we can only faintly see, or what John Piper calls "faith in future grace."[2] Faith is a function of hope; hope is future-oriented faith. Calvin defines faith as "a firm and certain knowledge of God's benevolence toward us, founded upon the truth of the freely given promise in Christ, both revealed to our minds and sealed upon our hearts through the Holy Spirit."[3] What is most significant in Calvin's definition is its God-centeredness. Faith is a firm knowledge of *God's* benevolence, his grace and kindness toward us. It is a knowledge that anchors us, especially in hard situations, because it pledges to us God's care now and in the future.

2 See John Piper, *The Purifying Power of Living by Faith in Future Grace* (Multnomah, 1995).

3 John Calvin, *Institutes of the Christian Religion*, ed. John T. McNeill, trans. Ford Lewis Battles, 2 vols., Library of Christian Classics 20–21 (Westminster John Knox, 2006), 3.2.7.

In the language of Hebrews, faith is the firm and certain "assurance of things hoped for" (Heb. 11:1). And hope is generated by God's character (as proven in the past) and God's promises—both of which are preserved for us in Scripture. This brings us to the Psalms. The psalmist prays,

> And take not the word of truth utterly out of my mouth,
> for my hope is in your rules. (Ps. 119:43)

> Those who fear you shall see me and rejoice,
> because I have hoped in your word. (119:74)

> I rise before dawn and cry for help;
> I hope in your words. (119:147)

Appropriately, he makes God's words the object of his hope because these words of the Lord declare who God is and make promises about who he will be for those who are in relationship with him. When we come to Scripture, we must approach it with faith-filled hope that the things written in it will be fulfilled in and for us. In fact, faith and hope may be the most basic orientation to God's word. Obedience springs from faith. Perseverance in following the Scriptures feeds on hope. The greatest honor we can give God and his word is to believe.

Practices

Keeping

By far the most common response to God's word in Psalm 119 is captured by the word *keep*. Roughly thirty times the psalmist declares his commitment to "keep" the law. He writes, for example,

> Blessed are those who keep his testimonies. (Ps. 119:2)
>
> Oh that my ways may be steadfast
> in keeping your statutes! (119:5)
>
> I will keep your statutes. (119:8)

"To keep" is literally "to guard" or "keep close watch" over something. When applied to God's word, the psalmist is saying that he diligently and vigilantly seeks to observe the law. He won't allow the law to be mistreated, undervalued, or disregarded in his own life. In essence, to keep is to obey. The psalmist's singular resolution is to obey the law. This is captured in the synonyms he uses to convey this commitment. He will observe it (119:34, 146), do it (119:166), walk in it (119:1, 3), live according to it (119:85), run in the way of it (119:32), and incline his heart to perform it (119:112).

As Christians, we have to be careful to highlight that our loving obedience to God's commands is enabled by the Holy Spirit. This is one of the promises of the new covenant, that God will put his Spirit in us and cause us to walk in his statutes and be careful to obey his rules (Ezek. 36:27). Having said this, we must also avoid overcomplicating the Christian life and, specifically, our relationship to God's word. Our fundamental responsibility toward Scripture is to obey it. To read Scripture without the unwavering commitment to obey and follow it is to profoundly misread Scripture. If Scripture is indeed God's word, then any other response or orientation to it is a subtle denial of his lordship.

Meditation

As a consequence of his love and delight, the psalmist meditates on the law. In fact, this is a connection he makes explicitly:

> I will lift up my hands toward your commandments,
> which I love,
> and I will meditate on your statutes. (Ps. 119:48)

Elsewhere, he exclaims,

> Oh how I love your law!
> It is my meditation all the day. (119:97)

He praises God's commands, which he loves, and he meditates on this object of his joy "all the day." Meditation is not some sort of mystical experience but rather "careful, prolonged contemplation, poring over the Scriptures eagerly to know God in his self-revelation and to live unto him faithfully."[4] Meditation consists of reading and/or hearing, memorizing, pondering, and continually reciting God's word.[5] In meditating, Scripture fills our thoughts and becomes our constant conversation partner throughout the day.

4 Bruce K. Waltke and Fred G. Zaspel, *How to Read and Understand the Psalms* (Crossway, 2023), 14.

5 Willem A. VanGemeren, *Psalms*, in *Psalms–Song of Songs*, vol. 5 in *The Expositor's Bible Commentary*, ed. Frank E. Gaebelein (Zondervan, 2007), 55.

Remembrance

Delight-filled meditation helps to cultivate remembrance. Several times in our psalm, the writer pledges that he will not "forget" God's law:

> I will delight in your statutes;
> I will not forget your word. (Ps. 119:16)
>
> I will never forget your precepts,
> for by them you have given me life. (119:93)
>
> I am small and despised,
> yet I do not forget your precepts. (119:141)

To forget is not about having a temporary memory lapse. Instead, forgetting has to do with neglecting our duties. This was the case when Israel regularly "forgot" what the Lord did for them in Egypt (Deut. 4:9; 6:12; 8:14) and then acted ungratefully, and even gave themselves over to idols. Rather than being faithful to the covenant, they "forgot" the Lord. Forgetting takes many other forms in Scripture: abandoning temple worship (Isa. 65:11), violating religious and social obligations (Ezek. 22:12), and trusting in wealth (Hos. 8:14).[6]

Remembering, on the other hand, requires calling to mind what God has said and done and then devoting ourselves to living in light of those things. When the psalmist says that he will not forget God's law, he is declaring that he will not neglect to

6 Leslie C. Allen, "שׁכח," in *The New International Dictionary of Old Testament Theology and Exegesis*, ed. Willem A. VanGemeren, 5 vols. (Zondervan Academic, 2012), 4:104.

give due attention to it. He will store it in his heart (Ps. 119:11). He will cling to it (119:31). He will not stray from it (119:51, 102, 110, 157) nor forsake it (119:87) by believing there is better wisdom or joy or fulfillment elsewhere. Remembrance requires diligence. Its basic meaning is to "pay attention to."[7] The one who vows not to forget God's word is the person who commits himself to knowing and living the Scriptures rather than hoping to lazily lapse into greater devotion. Paying attention to God's word requires not only that we give time to it but also that we have, as our default, the inclination to heed it.

God's word is the gift that gives so many other gifts. May we receive it as grace from the loving heart of God. Let me close with this charge from the great Reformer Heinrich Bullinger:

> Let us therefore in all things believe the word of God delivered to us by the scriptures. Let us think that the Lord himself, which is the very living and eternal God, doth speak to us by the scriptures. Let us for evermore praise the name and goodness of him, who hath vouchedsafe so faithfully, fully, and plainly to open to us, miserable mortal men, all the means how to live well and holily. To him be praise, honour, and glory forever more. Amen.[8]

7 Thomas E. McComiskey, "*zakar*," in *Theological Wordbook of the Old Testament*, ed. R. Laird Harris, Gleason L. Archer Jr., and Bruce K. Waltke, 2 vols. (Moody, 2003), 1:241.

8 Henry Bullinger, *The Decades of Henry Bullinger*, 2 vols., ed. Thomas Harding (Reformation Heritage, 2004), 1:56–57.

Acknowledgments

As with most books, this one was greatly helped along by the kindness and generosity of others. I am grateful for the support of Talbot School of Theology and Biola University for providing a sabbatical leave, which allowed me to focus on this project. Thanks to Charlie Trimm and Daniel Kim for resources and help in understanding some Hebrew terms. Thanks also to Hank Voss for always passing along resources and for many words of encouragement. My gratitude goes to all those who gave feedback on titles and graciously endured my many bad suggestions—Jordan Barrett, Adam and Anna Day, Arvind and Karisa Balaram, Jeremy Treat, Steve Pardue, and my kids, Zoe, Eli, and Ezra. Finally, I thank my wife, Melissa, for her feedback on the whole book and, even more so, for her enthusiastic support. This book is dedicated to her, a woman who truly loves, lives, and ministers God's word faithfully.

Appendix

Scriptural Prayers About Scripture

EACH OF THE MAIN CHAPTERS in this book ends with a song of praise or petition for God's gifts given to us through the gift of Scripture. Every song is directed toward God and his word and thus follows the Bible's own way of exalting the God of the Scriptures and the Scriptures of the one true God. One unmistakable thing you notice as you read Psalm 119 is that the psalmist depends on God to truly understand his word and to know by experience its benefits. We are no different. Therefore, prayer becomes essential in our daily engagement with Scripture. That being the case, it would be helpful to have some sort of template for the kinds of prayers we ought to pray concerning Scripture. Thankfully, we have Psalm 119, which provides us with a number of prayers and petitions that lay the pattern for our own praying. Without expanding on each one, here is a list of the kinds of prayers that we can and should pray. I've left out specific prayers of praise (e.g., 119:7, 171, 172) since the whole psalm is one extended praise.

Prayers for Our Hearts

The psalmist recognizes that he is always in need of God's help if he is to delight in and stay faithful to God's word.

Oh that my ways may be steadfast
in keeping your statutes! (119:5)

Let me not wander from your commandments! (119:10)

Open my eyes, that I may
behold wondrous things out of your law. (119:18)

Help me stay on the path of your commands. (119:35 CSB)

Incline my heart to your testimonies,
and not to selfish gain! (119:36)

May my heart be blameless in your statutes,
that I may not be put to shame! (119:80)

Prayers That Appeal to Our Faithfulness to God's Word

"The Lord takes pleasure in those who fear him" (Ps. 147:11). Therefore, the psalmist prays in hope that the Lord will show him favor in light of his fidelity to God's law.

I will keep your statutes;
do not utterly forsake me! (119:8)

Take away from me scorn and contempt,
for I have kept your testimonies. (119:22)

I cling to your testimonies, O LORD;
let me not be put to shame! (119:31)

I am yours; save me,
for I have sought your precepts. (119:94)

Look on my affliction and deliver me,
for I do not forget your law. (119:153)

Consider how I love your precepts!
Give me life according to your steadfast love. (119:159)

Seek your servant,
for I do not forget your commandments. (119:176)

Prayers for Understanding and Insight

True understanding of God's word is a gift from God, not solely the possession of the highly educated. Thus, the psalmist goes straight to the Author, asking for insight into the Author's words.

Teach me your statutes! (119:12, 26, 64, 66, 68, 108, 124, 135)

Hide not your commandments from me! (119:19)

Make me understand the way of your precepts. (119:27)

Teach me, O LORD, the way [or "meaning"] of your statutes. (119:33)

Give me understanding, that I may keep your law
 and observe it with my whole heart. (119:34)

Give me understanding, that I may learn your
 commandments. (119:73)

Give me understanding,
 that I may know your testimonies! (119:125)

Give me understanding according to your word! (119:169)

Give me understanding, that I may live. (119:144)

Never take the word of truth from my mouth.
 (119:43 CSB)

Teach me good judgment and discernment,
 for I rely on your commands. (119:66 CSB)

Prayers That Others Would Honor God's Word

Those who love God's word desire that others would love it as well. It is fitting that one prays for the word of the Lord to be honored (see 2 Thess. 3:1).

Let those who fear you turn to me,
 that they may know your testimonies. (119:79)

It is time for the LORD to act,
 for your law has been broken. (119:126)

Prayers Holding God to His Scriptural Promises

To hold God to his promises is not presumptuous but rather an act of faith. God is faithful to his promises given in his word, and in recalling those promises in prayer, we are drawing attention to his great faithfulness.

> Give me life according to your word! (119:25, 107)

> Strengthen me according to your word! (119:28)

> Confirm to your servant your promise,
> that you may be feared. (119:38)

> Let your steadfast love comfort me
> according to your promise to your servant. (119:76)

> Let your mercy come to me, that I may live;
> for your law is my delight. (119:77)

> Uphold me according to your promise, that I may live,
> and let me not be put to shame in my hope! (119:116)

> Keep steady my steps according to your promise. (119:133)

Prayers for the Removal of External Obstacles to Obedience

While no external enemy can make us disobey God's word, there may be obstacles that keep us from living out and enjoying his commands to the full (e.g., persecution). Praying for the removal of these barriers is not necessarily an act of weakness.

Deal bountifully with your servant,
  that I may live and keep your word. (119:17)

Redeem me from man's oppression,
  that I may keep your precepts. (119:134)

May we pray this way. And as we do, may God cause us to truly know and love the Scriptures—his gift that gives us so many other gifts.

General Index

Scripture Index

"While qualified lay people can currently preach in the Church, they are prohibited from offering the homily at Mass. Heille and his colleagues, in the spirit of the Synod on Synodality, authored this proposal on lay eucharistic preaching. Informative and grounded in Church teaching, this treatise is an indispensable resource to those committed to understanding the canonical, theological, and pastoral considerations. In response to this proposal, the Vatican has acknowledged the issue and the need for deliberations. As the authors urge, the current gap should not be pitched as competition between laity and clergy. The treatises invite us, more importantly, to reflect on who we are as Church, how our baptism imparts responsibilities and charisms to all the faithful to proclaim the kingdom of God, and how we serve and help each other on this journey. Such reflections foster our imagination of the synodal eucharistic pulpit as a community in a context of adaptation of the liturgy over time."

—Carolyn Woo, former president and CEO of Catholic Relief Services

"Guided by Pope Francis's vision of the future synodal Church, Dominican Gregory Heille has gathered a veritable symphony of expert voices on lay preaching. In this important and timely topic, these preachers and teachers leave no stone unturned for an interrogation of the present state of Christian proclamation, while constructing an artful path forward: from a theology of ministry for lay eucharistic preaching, to a New Testament basis for such homiletics, toward an exploration of genuine, charismatic witness of the prophetic for the twenty-first century. Be ready to take a long-awaited, deep breath into the labor of the Spirit! This text will set the gold standard on a long-awaited exploration on lay preaching for years to come."

—Guerric DeBona, OSB, Saint Meinrad Seminary and School of Theology